SO-AUS-694

Enneatypes in
Psychotherapy

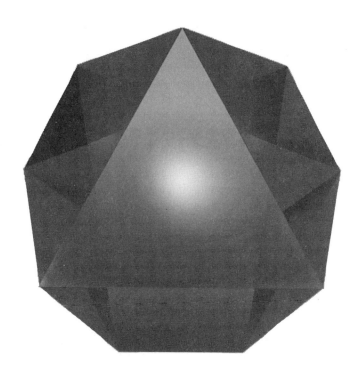

NZupold

Enneatypes In Psychotherapy

Selected Transcripts of the
First International Symposium
on the Personality Enneagrams

Pueblo Acantilado, Spain
December 1993

Claudio Naranjo, M.D.,
editor and research director

Translations by: Ana Serrano
and Cynthia Merchant

Hohm Press
Prescott, Arizona
1995

Hohm Press
P.O. Box 2501
Prescott, AZ, 86302

Layout, Typography and Cover Design:
Shukyo Lin Rainey

Copyright 1995 by Claudio Naranjo, M.D.
All rights reserved.
No part of this book may be used or reproduced in any manner
for public or private use without the written permission of the publisher,
except in the case of quotes embodied in critical articles or reviews.

Library of Congress number: 94-077115
ISBN: 0-934252-47-5

Manufactured in the United States of America
First Printing, January 1995

Dedication

To my students
especially to those whose words
are in these pages,
and to those
who gave their efforts
to recording, transcription and translation.

Other books by Claudio Naranjo

How To Be

Gestalt Therapy: The Attitude & Practice
of an Atheoretical Experientialism

The Healing Journey

The One Quest

The Psychology of Meditation

La Angonia del Patriarcado

El Niño Dinno y el Héroe

Gestalt Sin Fronteras

Songs of Enlightenment

Ennea-type Structures

Character and Neurosis, An Integrative View

$\mathcal{C}ontents$

Foreword

There seems to be an ongoing debate amongst "spiritual seekers" as to the need for (over and against indulgence in) deep inner
work as the foundation and prerequisite for expanded or higher
consciousness as a living and stable condition. Many people feel,
fuelled by their well-meaning but naive spiritual teachers, that it is
simply enough to affirm the ultimate reality, and voilà, enlightenment is bound to dawn . . . and quickly besides.

I suppose if we weren't in the vehicles we are in, that something of this nature might be possible—but even then I doubt it.
The obstacles that lie in our path due to the unobserved and unac-
knowledged dynamics of personality (as this word is used in this
excellent book) cannot be leapt over or dissipated merely by wishing them to be out of the way, no matter how sincere this wishing.
Our underworld will not go away, no matter how much we focus
on our upperworld (so to speak). In order to be "spiritually mature"
creatures, we need to deal with who we are now, on every level,
just as we are, not in some ideal or abstract projection, no matter
how philosophically correct (p.c.) our projection may be.

The use, or should I say the proper use, of the Enneatype system is an invaluable tool towards this end of "spiritual maturity"
(and towards basic human sanity and maturity besides—no mean

feat!). The more educated we are, not relying solely on the therapist to do all our work for us, the more likely it is that such maturity will become true of us—not simply a momentary experience
that fades after an hour or a day, but an abiding, integral condition
of our lives. This book, *Enneatypes In Psychotherapy*, is not only
of vital necessity to any professional wishing to correctly understand and use the Enneatype system in his or her work, but can also
provide personal insight and value for anyone involved in true
transformational work-on-self. Dr. Naranjo is one of the foremost
practitioners and teachers of this system, and his work is one of the
best sources of accurate data.

Let me emphasize again, in different words: On the path there
is no substitute for the need to resolve and heal the wounds that,
unhealed and unresolved, effectively make it impossible to truly
progress! Unfortunately for the vast majority of "spiritual seekers,"
the illusion of progress is not, and never will be, progress itself.
Claudio's work is a great gift to earnest practitioners—those for
whom the vast field of their personal/mechanical manifestations is
a treasure of opportunities for discovery and transformation.

I have known Claudio for over ten years. His integrity, and his
more-than-extraordinary depth and breadth of knowledge, make
him one of the most vital spokespeople for a sound system of self-
work. Hohm Press is delighted to be able to offer *Enneatypes In
Psychotherapy* as our own way of confronting such a crucial need
in today's deeply struggling societies—this need being to clearly
address the strategies of ego that keep us defined by a closeminded
and depressed, rather than an open and expressive, life. These
days, more than ever, the few serious students of these ideas are a
bright light in a sea of darkness. The flippant rhetoric of so many
so-called "students of the work" needs to be moderated by honest
work-on-self. And the data in this book, and Dr. Naranjo's work in
general, deserve a wise, but more importantly, a dedicated perusal
and use.

Lee Lozowick
Prescott, AZ,
10 May 1994

Preface

When I taught protoanalysis in 1971-72 as part of my work with the groups that became the core of SAT INSTITUTE in Berkeley, I was explicitly declaring that this was something for "personal consumption" only. However, during the last ten years or so, as the enneagrams of fixations and passions are no longer an esoteric secret, I have taught mostly psychotherapists interested not only in their ongoing personal development but appreciative of the considerable influence that protoanalysis has had in their professional work.

Last December, when I accepted the position of coordinator of an international symposium among some of my students, I experienced the event as a sort of punctuation mark signaling the entry of the personality enneagrams into the professional world.

This book is an echo of that event—although the material that I have selected here is specifically relevant to psychotherapy as distinct from contributions in other areas, such as psychological testing, personality theory or education.

The first entry in this volume is a transcript of my opening talk at the symposium. Though an exception to the overall theme of "enneatypes and psychotherapy," I think it is appropriate as a prelude to the rest of the materials that saw the light during that five-day meeting.

The second chapter contains the observations of the Italian psychoanalyst, Luisa Giungi, on how her acquaintance with the psychology of enneatypes has reflected on her work, particularly in regard to the understanding and handling of transference.

The third chapter, by Suzana Stroke, contains the account of one of the world's more experienced practitioners of the Quadrinity (formerly Fischer-Hoffman) Process. She explains what she has learned concerning the best way of approaching the different enneatypes in the context of the Quadrinity Process approach to the remedial education of love.

Chapter 4 is a transcript of a round-table discussion among nine psychotherapists—each of them the voice of one particular personality style. My proposed theme to them for this meeting was that of sharing observations and insights in regard to the therapeutic opportunities or difficulties that arise in their work with people with the different characters.

In contrast to the above inquiry, which was carried out by a small group of speaking participants, the inquiry on dysfunctional thinking that is the subject of Chapter 5 was a larger group venture—the result of the work of some 200 people divided into 27 teams.

A last brief chapter in this collection is, along with this preface, the only part of the book that did not originate at the Personality Enneagrams '93 Symposium. I have written it specifically for inclusion here—mostly in view to making a more direct contribution than that of having been a stimulus to others.

I imagine that this book will appeal especially to those whose work is to help others psychologically, yet I would be very pleased if, besides becoming a professional's book, it would interest also those whose concern is helping themselves.

Claudio Naranjo, M.D.
Berkeley, CA
April 1994

Chapter 1

OPENING TALK
AT THE FIRST INTERNATIONAL SYMPOSIUM
ON THE PERSONALITY ENNEAGRAMS

by CLAUDIO NARANJO, M.D.

Juanjo (Dr. Juan José Albert) has already told the story of this meeting. It was his idea and thus his merit, along with that of the organizers. I wasn't too attracted by the idea at first, but I thought that it would be a good way to do something further along the lines of what we have been doing throughout the years. In my workshops, along with what I do know I have always admitted what I *don't* know. Thus, these workshops have always been occasions for learning together, of inquiring into and sharing on certain issues in a spirit of going a little further in our understanding, of clarifying things that were not completely clear. So, from the beginning, I thought that this meeting would be an occasion for some of that workshop spirit (a different spirit from that of conferences) —a more intimate spirit, more oriented to learning and getting to know each other in view of the intrinsic benefits involved, rather than out of dehumanized, purely scientific, if not narcissistic motivations.

As time went by, however, another motivation for holding this meeting was added. Before becoming known for the various things with which I am associated today, I was a personality researcher. I left Chile for the U.S. at a time when I was feeling frustrated with what help I could offer as a psychoanalyst. Before meeting Fritz Perls (the first therapeutic experience to touch me deeply, making it possible for me to do things for others), I had dedicated a considerable time to personality research, especially to mathematical studies: factor analytic studies of personality and values. Therefore, it was only natural that, after becoming familiar with the Enneagram, I have wanted to motivate other people to carry out psychometric validation and other research. This conference has served as stimulus for speeding up projects, in many different subjects, that various persons had undertaken.

There will be a third element in our meeting: a sharing of research different from the two kinds I have described. The presentation of this different research will take the form of performances, especially in the case of Ramón Resino. Ramón has promised to implement something that has been an old dream of mine, something we intended to do in Bilbao years ago, that is, a seminar focusing on the enneatypes in Spanish drama. This dream never went beyond making a list of works to study, until now. A single person, a theater director and actor with a great culture in drama, is volunteering to do, by himself, something that could well be enough for a whole conference, if we had time for it. Because there are so many activities, we are going to have to narrow his contribution to two nights—one night for a global vision (I have asked him to provide a panoramic vision from the Greeks to modern Spanish theater, with some close-ups, monologues and dialogues which he will perform with his collaborators); the other night to "La Casa de Bernarda Alba" by García Lorca, a work which has nine characters who, as Ramón plans to explain, correspond to each enneatype. I expect that, aside from learning something further about the enneatypes through literature (which as a rule goes so much deeper

2

than psychology), we may find the impact of Garcia Lorca's tragedy meaningful.

I have been telling Graciela Figueroa for years that someday I would like her to dance the Enneagram for us. As you know, she is not only a prestigious dancer, but also a body-worker. So I hope that her knowledge of movement, together with her art, will bring us something good.

And José Luis Pérez. . . I thought he could offer us something like what he did in the last SAT program when I suggested that he not only teach us the traditional dances, but that he do so with emphasis on the psychological atmosphere involved in each, which is to say the atmosphere of the corresponding enneatypes. This also turned out to be an excessively ambitious project. For this meeting, therefore, it will take the form of a simple demonstration—a talk punctuated by illustrations of dance, music and lyric—instead of an occasion for a lot of dancing.

Let me say something concerning my part—the workshop component of our Symposium. One of Juanjo's motivations, when he suggested the Symposium to me, was to refine the descriptions of the subtypes a little, and I think this will also interest many others. We have seen how, in the workshops, some are more represented than others. While certain subtypes are sufficiently represented (type IV, type VI, and sometimes II), we are delighted when some type VIII subtype can be illustrated. In workshops I have lately stopped resorting to my own descriptions of the types, instead bringing together people with a similar character and asking them to produce descriptions themselves. These have turned out to be as good as those that can be found in any book, or even better, in a certain way, since they have the freshness of what has just been discovered by people who are struggling with them. But, commonly we do not have sufficient people to produce illustrative group formulations in some of the subtypes. So, I hope that with the attendance of about two hundred people, as we have here, we will have the occasion of taking a good look at this descriptive aspect of the personality variants.

Another issue for this workshop component is that of therapeutical change. This is a matter we have been inquiring into not only from the point of view of the traditional model, but also from the point of view of these ideas I launched some twenty years ago concerning movement in the Enneagram. Now it has become a matter of dogma that a personality shift in the directions of the arrows spells out pathology while a movement against the arrows is therapeutic. By now I have seen plenty of exceptions to either rule, and I am inclined to think that both shifts are part of integration and either of them may involve suffering. We will explore this idea together as we look into the broader issue of change over time. I have prepared some processes for systematic inquiry and for comparing observations.

A third matter we are going to inquire into is that of "crazy ideas," i.e. the cognitive aspect of the ego (according to the theory, this is the aspect of implicit delusion underlying the emotional aspect). In the domain of what I have been calling "crazy ideas" there is a certain group of "crazy ideas" that are inner imperatives, corresponding to what are called scripts in transactional psychology. That is why I have asked Antonio Ferrara to give a lecture that is meant to provide a stimulus to our group inquiry into the thought tendencies that are linked to character.

I also want to invite you to inquire into how one deals with difficult people outside psychotherapy, or outside the situation of having undertaken a responsibility of spiritual assistance. We, as therapists, are in a role of being *for others* most of our life, that is to say our working life. At other times, in social life and also in working life, we need to find a way of being benevolent with others and with ourselves too. In view of this, how do we act in the face of difficult people of the different character types? I believe we have all had some important experiences in which we really discovered what to do with a particular type VIII tyrant, for instance, or how to deal with a particular kind of demanding type IV, or how to handle a particular form of seduction. Through experience we have all acquired some clarity. In the spirit of a Symposium, therefore, I would like to promote a good harvest of insights that may be of use to us all. So, my part in this Symposium (in the strictest sense of the word) will be to foster inquiry into what we all know, in order to share it and reach certain group conclusions.

Another of the elements that I thought would constitute a rich contribution to this meeting would be the presentation of what results we have now from a long-standing scrutiny of Balzac's *Human Comedy*. Again, we will not have the time to do this in full detail, yet the illustrative excerpts corresponding to the three subtypes of a given personality style will be read in small group meetings among those for whom they are most relevant. Balzac expressed the ambition and the conviction of having achieved an exhaustive description of human characters. It has been said of him that, more than a man of letters, he was a scientist at a time when psychology had not yet arisen as a science. (He frequently compared himself to Cuvier.) His description of characters, not only in the different social levels of Parisian life, but also in the country, in military life, etc., was intended to be exhaustive; and perhaps from our point of view, it is.

About ten years ago I conducted some seminars, in Brazil and Spain, in which I distributed among the participants nearly a hundred novels comprising Balzac's monumental *Human Comedy*. Each participant was asked to study one particular novel and report on its main characters. This material has been reviewed mainly by Annie Chevreaux and Carmen Durán who have checked the diagnoses by subtypes and made sure that all the important traits were documented by quotation of the relevant passages. I now hope this Symposium will allow us to complete this excellent work. Only a final step is missing: the confirmation from those who embody the corresponding subtype that these selected characters reflect them properly. We intend to present you with distillates, perhaps by means of quotes from the novels, from Balzac's descriptions of the twenty-seven human types. Since this will not be done in our plenary sessions, but rather in a simultaneous meeting of the nine enneatype groups, we will then share together concerning the outcome of the discussions and later publish the material as an Addendum to the Symposium.

An important component of our program will be discussions in small groups. Another will be a series of *public* small group discussions—round tables. These lend themselves especially to the spirit of a symposium, which is to benefit from mutual stimulation and to bring together perceptions from differing points of view. Often, a discussion among a few people can do, in a short time, what is not so easily accomplished in a large group. One group will meet to discuss Forms of Transference, characteristic of the Enneagram types. I am using the term *transference* in the broad sense of the word, that of bringing to present life a form of relationship from the past, and will invite the discussants to examine not only the positive aspect, but the negative as well, thus broaching the huge issue of resistance.

Another more complex issue we will deal with is that of therapeutic relations. I have conducted several seminars (which some of you have attended years ago, here and in Brazil) on the multiple possibilities of relationship between the different character types: EI with EI, EI with EII, EI with EIII...EII with type EIII, EII with EIV . . . . In short, eighty-one possible encounters, each of which involves its own potential and its own difficulties, not only for family or social life, but especially in the situation of assisting someone's inner progress. This is beginning to be a privileged object of study in the U.S.A. where it has been established that, to a considerable extent, the success of psychotherapy lies on personality. So, we have organized a discussion with a representative from each character type so that the different perspectives can be checked against each other. (Of course some people will have more experience concerning specific relations among the characters.) Even though it is not possible to share, in a couple of hours, everything observed about all the types of relationship, we can at least get a general picture of what is involved on the issue and what deserves future research.

We will also have another round table discussion that will take as its subject the significance that the Enneagram has had for those who work with psychotherapy from the point of view of their respective specialties: transactional, body therapy, gestalt, etc.

Also, we have scheduled a discussion on enneatype awareness in professional, non-therapeutic relationships with people from spheres ranging from architecture and law, to hairdressing. (Thus, we have among us a sort of *Barbero de Sevilla*, only that he is not quite from Sevilla but from Alicante. We know through Rossini's opera and also through Alban Berg's *Wozzek*, which also has a barber as a central character, how the human world unfolds to the barber's eyes.) I look forward very much to this meeting and believe that it will be especially interesting because the participants have not been preparing for this event over the years, not even over the last few months. Instead, we have taken them by surprise and asked them to tell us what they know without having asked themselves previously; to look back on how this knowledge has influenced their lives and how without seeking to do so they have put the information to use.

We will also have a meeting intended to bring together perceptions on body structure, posture, gesture and physiognomy. Bioenergetics has described the tensional pattern of "body armor" in various characters, but from a point of view not identical to that of our characterology, and I think that it should provide inspiration for the formulation of the tensional models of the character types as we know them. The bioenergetic perspective will help, but it will also be desirable to bring to the issue a fresh vision that does not lean on anything beyond what an experienced body-worker has before him or her.

There will be a great many other contributions: on Rorschach responses, on graphology, on Hartmann's test of values, on the positive features of the enneatypes, on the behavior of the different character types in the Quadrinity Process, on reactions to the Bach flower remedies, animal identifications, and so forth.

Finally, Juanjo has asked me to do something special, something of a more spiritual nature, so we don't stick only to analytical matters. A few days ago I started thinking that it had to be something very special because it is the tenth anniversary of my work in the Latin world. I don't know how many of you know that I only taught in the U.S. for a year and a half. Then I decided not to continue, as an expression of disapproval toward some who regarded themselves to be endowed with the authority to write the first books about material that was not their own. Now the field is open, however, and I feel that our meeting signals the diffusion of protoanalysis to a larger community.

It only remains for me to hope the heavens will be kind to us. And, since I imagine that most of you believe, as I do, that the Universe is not only a machine, but that there is a consciousness that corresponds to ours, I propose that we stay silent for a moment to concentrate on an intention that our meeting be beneficial for everybody here and for the world that surrounds us.

Chapter 2

THE ENHANCING POWER OF
THE ENNEAGRAM OF THE PERSONALITY
IN THE PSYCHOANALYTIC WAY OF WORK

By LUISA GUINGI POWELL

I. SUMMARY

The project is to show the impact of the Enneagrams of the personality on the writer who has received psychoanalytic training and who is practicing as a Kleinian psychoanalytic psychotherapist.

The method by which the writer intends to proceed is by discussing briefly some of the basic instruments of the psychoanalytic way of working, such as the notion of mutative interpretation, that of the complete interpretation, and of the Kleinian approach and use of transference, relating it to the understanding offered by Protoanalysis and the mechanisms of defence of the various character structures.

The objective is to show that the dual aspect of extreme depth and synthesis of vision provided by the Enneagrams of the personality offer a unique opportunity of integrating and potentiating the psychoanalytic approach, which is not strong in its synthetic function, and not as specific in its capacity to go for the very root of the person's pathology.

I propose to report some excerpts from sessions with patients to illustrate how my way of working has been enormously helped and quickened in its efficacy by this new instrument of work.

II. INTRODUCTION

It is nearly a year and a half since I had the good fortune of meeting Claudio and learning about Protoanalysis and the enneatype structure of the personality. This encounter has had deep repercussions on myself as a person, and now on my work.

I must admit that the discovery at first was a shock: had I been wasting my time with twelve years of psychoanalysis? This was my first angry reaction. Yes, you have guessed, I am an angry type. Twelve years of analytical perfectioning, first Jungian and then Kleinian, had not done the trick! That was too bad. So I set to work again, this time my aim was to reduce my excessive severity, my need to control, and above all, to realize how my intuition had suffered from unconditional submission to reason.

Spontaneity began to loom at the horizon! The reassuring aspect among all these changes was that my work as a psychoanalyst improved and, more specifically, my capacity for psychoanalytic observation. Thanks to the teaching of the personality structures and their strategies and defences, I had acquired a new coherence and clarity, that previously had been lacking.

During an analytical session there are at times many possible themes that one may choose to take up, and from many different angles. It is possible and easy to be drawn into secondary problem areas. Protoanalysis helps to keep our attention on the primary root of the personality structure and its pathology. The domain of the personality is so vast that it cannot be totally investigated. It cannot therefore be said that an analysis has been completed.

Bion observed that, when people have finished analysis, their knowledge about themselves is greater than when they started, but it is probable that their psychic growth will be greater than the knowledge about themselves. This I believe to be true of my case because I can genuinely say that I have had a very enriching psychoanalytical experience, which has, in turn, generated considerable benefits and changes in my external life and circumstances. But, until I came across the enneatype structures of the personality and their mechanisms of defence, strategies, and virtues, my knowledge about myself was much more limited. This increased knowledge has brought about an expansion of consciousness, which is exactly, according to Bion, the aim of psychoanalytic treatment.

I would like to speak of the differences, to myself as a person and as an analyst, and of the differences in my approach to the material in the understanding of the patient. Starting from myself, I can say that now I have a calmer and clearer understanding, both of who I am, and of the people I work with. I can see, more quickly, their defence structure and what urges them to act as they do, which leaves me to concentrate on interpreting.

Bion recommends absence of memory or desire in the analyst's attitude to his/her patient. This is what I actually feel.

Another great advantage, I believe, is my having become better able to detect the unconscious model underlying the patient's behavior.

Protoanalysis offers the key to the reading of the wrong theory, the mistaken assumption underlying the patient's unconscious phantasies which are structuring not only his/her internal world, but also his/her relationship to external reality. As I will show later in my theoretical excursion, this is a key point in Kleinian theory.

III. SUMMARY OF THE THEORY

A. Interpretation and Transference

The interpretation is the fundamental technical instrument of psychoanalysis. It is, as Freud said, what makes conscious the unconscious: the individual needs precise information on himself and on what is happening to him and on what he is ignoring about himself, in order to understand his psychological reality. Analysis is the method that concerns itself with discovering and analyzing the transference. In this sense it can be said that the transference is, in itself, the illness.

Freud defined the transference as a general phenomenon, universal and spontaneous, which consists in joining the past with the present through a false connection which superimposes the original person (the past) on the present one. The superimposition of past on present is linked to persons and desires from the past which are not conscious for the subject and that give his or her conduct an irrational seal—the affect does not seem appropriate either in quality or in quantity to the real, actual situation.

Greenson (1967) says that the two fundamental traits of a transference reaction are that it is repetitive and inappropriate, that is, irrational. The more we mistake the past for the present, the more ill we are.

The relationship, doctor-patient, in the analytical setting, evidences the unfolding of the transference phenomenon. The patient is prepared to make an enormous effort in repeating, in the transference, the painful but ineluctable experiences from his past. It is the force of the desire and the stubborn hope of arriving somehow at a solution that leads to the repetition of the need, which, in the final instance make a psychoanalytic treatment possible.

B. Melanie Klein

In Freud's model, the transference is understood as a repetition of the past. Melanie Klein has a different model of transference. Her model rests basically on the existence of an internal world of objects in which the individual lives as fully as in the ex-

12

ternal world, and where transference appears as the externalization of the immediate present of the internal situation, not as a relic of the past.

In this sense the transference is seen more as an actualization of the present internal world, than a repetition of the past.

Meltzer (1978) tells us that, far from misleading us, transference is our compass, guiding us in the external world.

C. Unconscious Phantasy

The theory of unconscious phantasy, formalized by S.Isaacs in 1948, constitutes the backbone of Kleinian investigation and can be used to explain the transference. According to Isaacs, unconscious phantasy is an activity that is always present. If this is the case, we can interpret each time we grasp how unconscious phantasy is operating at a given moment. It is at this point that I see the usefulness of integrating Protoanalysis as the key to the understanding of the unconscious phantasy underlying all our communications. Beyond my speaking with faultless logic, beneath what I say, my phantasies exist at the level of a primary process. From this it follows that the transference is always alluded to, and is, to a variable degree, always present.

A basic postulate of Kleinian thought is that appropriate interpretation allays anxiety at the deep levels of the mind, and that this is a pre-requisite for analyzing the relation of the person's ego with reality.

A good interpretation, a complete interpretation, should take into account three different areas at the same time and show the essential identity of what happens in the consulting room with what is happening outside, and with what happened in the past. A complete interpretation should integrate these three levels: infantile conflict, present conflict, and transference. Only this kind of interpretation, which Strachey (1934) called "mutative interpretation," can bring about structural changes in the ego and break the vicious circle of neurosis.

I believe that Protoanalysis and the enneatype structures of the personality provide the pre-requisite for the best psychoanalytic work to be carried out according to my Kleinian training.

IV. THEORETICAL EXCURSION

During the first decade of this century, psychoanalysis had already gathered a number of theories and techniques which have remained to this day its foundation stones. After his experiments with hypnosis, Freud discovered a new theory, the theory of resistance. This led to a new technique—free association (which became the fundamental rule of psychoanalysis), which led to the theory of trauma, and that remembering gradually made way for the theory of sexuality. The conflict was no longer only between remembering and forgetting, but also between instinctive and repressive forces.

From that point on discoveries multiplied: infantile sexuality and the Oedipus complex, the unconscious with its laws and contents, the theory of transference, and so on. On this new context of discoveries, interpretation appears as a fundamental technical instrument and in complete agreement with the new hypothesis.

With the aim only of recovering a memory, neither the cathartic method, nor associative coercion had needed interpretation. Now it was different; it was now necessary to give individuals precise information on themselves—on what was happening to them and what they were ignoring, so that they would be able to understand their psychological reality. We call this *interpretation*: the instrument that makes conscious the unconscious.

In other words, during the first decade of this century, the theory of resistance was being vigorously extended in two directions. On the one hand, the unconscious (that which is resisted) was discovered, with its laws of condensation and displacement and its contents: the theory of libido. On the other hand, the theory of transference arose, that is, a precise way of defining the doctor-patient relationship (as resistance always occurs in terms of the relationship with the doctor).

The immediate repercussion on technique, which the theory of transference had, was a reformulation of the analytic relationship, which was now defined in rigorous and precise terms. The rigorous definition of the setting permitted, in turn, a greater precision in the appreciation of the transference phenomenon, as a stricter and more stable setting avoids its contamination and makes it clearer and more transparent. This was a slow process and continued after Freud.

V. TRANSFERENCE

Freud defined the transference as a general phenomenon, universal and spontaneous, which consists in joining the past with the present through a false connection, which superimposes the original person on the present one. The superimposition of past on present is linked to persons and desires from the past that are not conscious for the subject and that give his conduct an irrational seal—the affect does not seem appropriate either in quality or in quantity to the real, actual situation.

Transference, as a phenomenon of the Unconscious system, belongs to psychic reality, to phantasy, and not to factual reality. The two fundamental traits of a transference reaction (Greenson, 1967, p.155) are that it is repetitive and inappropriate, that is irrational. The psychic event is always a mixture of phantasy and reality.

We should consider, therefore, the transference as the irrational, the unconscious, the infantile in human conduct, co-existing with the rational, the conscious, and the adult in a complementary series.

Not everything is transference. As analysts we should discover the portion of it that exists in every mental act and every accompanying physical manifestation. Freud said that the transference is not an effect of analysis, rather, analysis is the method that concerns itself with discovering and analyzing the transference. In this sense it can be said that the transference is, in itself, the illness. The more we transfer the past to the present, the more we mistake the present for the past, the more ill we are—the more disturbed is our reality principle.

The other problem Freud posed in 1912 is the relation of transference to resistance. He said that the transference operates as resistance because it reactivates the memory (mostly blind and always painful), making it current and actual, at which point it ceases to be a memory. He also says that an enemy cannot be conquered *in absentia* or *in effigie*.

In 1920, in *Beyond the Pleasure Principle*, Freud asserts specificially that the transference is motivated by the compulsion to reap, and that the ego represses it to serve the pleasure principle. Repetition now becomes the explanatory principle of the transference. The transference now appears to be thoroughly serving the death instinct, that elemental and blind force that seeks a state of immobility and stagnation. Here Freud feels the drama of it, but does not understand that the transference is not a demonic impulse to repeat, rather that the analysand repeats because he/she is subject to his/her history, his or her past. The patient is prepared to make an enormous effort in repeating, in the transference, the painful but ineluctable experiences from his or her past. It is the force of desire and the stubborn hope of arriving somehow at a solution that leads to the repetition of the need which, in the final instance, makes psychoanalytic treatment possible.

For many years no one doubted that transference had its roots in repetition until Lacan, in 1964, questioned this hypothesis and broke the connection between repetition and transference.

In more recent years, other excellent scholars such as Meltzer, the Sandlers, and Merton Gill, also come to question the link between repetition and transference. In 1978, Meltzer wrote *The Kleinian Development.* In it he follows, from a very original point of view, the great arc that goes from Freud to Melanie Klein, and from her to Bion.

Meltzer suggests that Freud, always working on neurophysiological lines in accordance with the spirit of his times (which sought to place psychoanalysis among the sciences capable of explaining the facts of nature), could only understand the transference as a repetition of the past.

Melanie Klein's model rests basically on the existence of an internal world of objects, in which the individual lives as fully as in the external world, and in which transference appears as the externalization of the immediate present of the internal situation, not as a relic of the past.

Bion's model finally considers the mind as a thinking apparatus, in which the basic dilemma is between truth and lies, starting from the emotional experience of life in which emotion is placed at the very heart of meaning. In this epistemological model, relations in the internal world engender meaning, and, consequently, ". . . all of our external relationships have a certain transference quality in the sense that they derive meaning from what exists in our internal world . . ." (Meltzer, 1981, p.183).

From Meltzer's presentation we are induced to think of the transference more as an actualization of the present internal world, than as a repetition of the past. Moreover, what Meltzer is telling us is that, far from misleading us, transference is our compass, guiding us in the external world.

A. Melanie Klein. The Origins of Transference

Klein maintains that the transference operates throughout life and influences all human relations. In analysis, the past is gradually relived. The deeper we go into the unconscious and the further back we can take the analytic process, the greater will be our comprehension of the transference (Klein, 1975, vol.3, p.48).

The basic assertion of this paper is that the early stages of development appear in the transference as " memories in feelings," and that we can, therefore, grasp and reconstruct them. The transference is a fitting, sensible, and trustworthy instrument with which to reconstruct the early past. Klein reconstructs a great deal.

B. Transference and Unconscious Phantasy

The theory of unconscious phantasy formalized by S. Isaacs in 1948 (*International Journal of Psychoanalysis*) constitutes the backbone of Kleinian investigation and can be used to explain the transference. According to Isaacs, unconscious phantasy is an activity that is always present. If this is the case, we can interpret each time we grasp how unconscious phantasy is operating at a given moment. This gives the analyst greater freedom to interpret without the need for a rupture in the discourse, as Lacan, for example, would say, because the phantasy underlines the most coherent manifest content. Beyond my speaking with faultless logic, beneath what I say, my phantasies exist at the level of a primary process.

As a typical expression of the Unconscious system, unconscious phantasy always operates at some level, with primary objects and with that portion of unsatisfied libido that has recharged them via regression. From this it follows that the transference is always alluded to, and is to a variable degree always present. This is why M. Klein states that the transference operates not only if the patient alludes directly or indirectly to the analyst, but permanently, and that the issue is to know how to detect it.

> My conception of transference as rooted in the earliest stages of development and in deep layers of the unconscious is much wider and it entails a technique by which from the whole material presented the unconscious elements of the transference are deducted. (Klein, 1975)

I think these characteristics are the patrimony of Klein's way of working, of her style: the continuous action of unconscious phantasy, the interpretation of the negative transference, and the existence of early transference. The convergence of these three factors explains why we Kleinians interpret the transference more than others. A basic postulate of Kleinian thought is that appropriate interpretation allays anxiety at the deep levels of the mind and that this is a pre-requisite for analyzing the relation of the child's ego with reality.

Furthermore, M. Klein thinks that the child's ego and its relation to external reality are a gradual becoming, which is the result of analytical work.

I believe this very precise statement illustrates what M. Klein means by direct and deep interpretation together with her strategy to get in contact with the unconscious. Here we can notice her difference from Freud in her perception of the meaning of transference and the function of interpretation.

Where Freud holds an attitude of confident caution, Klein holds the opposite view—that the rapport with the patient is obtained only by interpreting.

A good interpretation, a complete interpretation, should take into account three different areas at the same time, and show the essential identity of what happens in the consulting room with what is happening outside, and what happened in the past.

If we take only one of these areas, as if the other two did not exist, then we no longer operate with the theory of transference. A complete interpretation should integrate these three levels: infantile conflict, present conflict, and transference.

C. The Mutative Interpretation

In 1934, James Strachey wrote *The Nature of the Therapeutic Action of Psychoanalysis*, which is one of the most valuable works in analytical literature. In this work, Strachey makes use of M. Klein's notion of the continuous play of projection and introjection on the part of the psychic apparatus in the building up of the ego. He demonstrates, simultaneously, the mechanism of the illness and that of the cure.

Strachey speaks of the "vicious circle" of neurosis and of the "virtuous circle" of the cure. He observes that the vicious circle is created when hate is projected into the object, which then is perceived as dangerous because of the hatred projected into it. This compels a reinforcement of hate as a defence. A virtuous circle takes place when, each time, the object becomes more protective and good, thus enabling introjection of love, which in turn promotes projection of love.

Strachey observes that cure is possible if the analyst manages to break this neurotic vicious circle that perpetuates infantile conflicts and impedes the growth of the individual. If we break this vicious circle, Strachey concludes, development would be reestablished spontaneously. In order to do so, Strachey says that the analyst, at the beginning of the process, puts himself or herself in the position of the analysand's super-ego and acts as an auxiliary super-ego, not with a view to demolish it, but to operate from an advantageous position, thus enabling a correction of the distorted perception. In fact, the analytic setting gives the patient the singular opportunity of projecting and seeing that these projections do not correspond to reality, in that the analyst responds with an impartial attitude. But, this alone is not enough. The pressure of the infantile super-ego (and in general of the conflict) makes the tendency to misunderstand real experience very great. The difference between the archaic super-ego and the auxiliary super-ego is labile and aleatory, and too easily the patient can find ways in phantasy or reality to subsume the new super-ego into the old one. However, the analyst has at his or her disposal a singular instrument to prevent that superimposition, and that is interpretation.

Strachey knows full well that the idea of interpretation is ambiguous and charged with affective connotations, if not irrational and magical ones. This is why he tries to specify it with his concept of mutative interpretation. Strachey calls an interpretation *mutative* when it produces structural changes. He says that it consists of two moments which can also occur simultaneously. The key of the theory is rooted in the analysand's awareness of two things: an instinctive impulse and an object unsuited to that impulse. The analyst must reemerge from the interpretative process as a real figure. This is what matters most to Strachey, that the analysand can become aware of the distance between his or her archaic object and the actual one.

The two phases of the mutative interpretation have to do with anxiety. The first phase liberates it, the second resolves it. When the anxiety is already manifest, the second phase should be administered. Strachey seems to advance here, in a certain way, Anna Freud's thought, who in 1936 will say that interpretative work has to fluctuate continually between the id and the ego.

Strachey observes three characteristics of the mutative interpretation: immediacy, specificity, and progressivity. An interpretation is immediate when it relates to an emotion that the analysand experiences in the here and now. (In other words, the interpretation should always bear on the point of urgency as Klein repeatedly indicates.) An interpretation is specific if it is detailed and concrete, a point Kris (1951) underlines when he recalls the necessity of attending to the preconscious links of the material. In fact, as long as we do not manage to focus the interpretation on relevant details, we can never expect a mutative effect. The interpretation should adapt itself exactly to what is happening; it should be delineated and concrete. Last, the mutative interpretation must act progressively, by well-graded steps, because otherwise either the first phase will not be reached, or the second will become impossible.

One final important point is Strachey's evaluation of the extra-transference interpretation. He demonstrates that the essential difference between transference interpretation and extra-transference interpretation is that only in the transference interpretation is the object of the id-impulse present.

It is difficult for the extra-transference interpretation to reach the point of urgency and, even if it managed to do so, it would always be problematic for the analysand to establish the difference between the real absent and that of his/her phantasy. An extra-transference interpretation cannot therefore be mutative. Only transference interpretation can be mutative. In this way, Strachey provides the theoretical principles for Freud's wise reflection that one cannot conquer an enemy *in absentia* or *in effigie*.

VI. WILHELM REICH AND ANNA FREUD

Freud, Ferenczi, Abraham, and Jones constructed a theory of character but not a theory of character defences as Reich did (see Reich, 1933). Reich had the great merit of integrating the instinctual explanation, that is the libido theory, with a theory of character defences.

On two issues Reich went further than Freud. First, he emphasized character structure. What was for Freud, in his technical writings, *psychic surface* (and later the ego) is *character* for Reich: not only the ego, but the operative forms of the ego that configure character. The second issue was the systematization of the technique, which is the other very important contribution of Reich. He warned against a merely intuitive attitude by basing himself on metapsychological and economical principles. He introduced the idea that technique is not sufficient; it is necessary to have a strategy.

Reich suggested a strategy for the analysis of the whole personality, that is, the analysis of character as resistance. His theory of character implies that the symptoms of neurosis in the adult are a consequence of the neurotic character and appear when the characterological armor begins to crack. The aggregate of character traits forms, for Reich, the character armor which operates as the main defence in the analysis. This armor has a definite economic function since it serves to dominate external stimuli and internal or instinctive stimuli.

Just as I have been evolving a defensive strategy that crystallizes in the character trait, my analyst has to provide himself or herself with a counterposed strategy, and to know how to select the material, centering the task on the multiple transference meanings of the character resistances.

Reich's emphasis on the operative forms of the ego that configure structure opened the way for the work of Anna Freud that followed: *The Ego and the Mechanisms of Defence* (1936).

In this famous book, Anna Freud gathered up Reich's ideas and further contributed to the improvement and natural development of the analytic process by postulating that the analyst's task consists basically in reaching an equilibrium, moving like a pendulum between the analysis of the ego and the analysis of the id.

Anna Freud told us that there is transference not only of positive and negative impulses, of love and hate, of instincts and affects, but also of defences. The transference of the id is felt by the patient as extraneous to his/her adult personality. The transference of defences repeats in the actuality of the analysis the old infantile models of ego functioning.

Reich did not develop a full range of character structures, nor did Anna Freud manage to bring together a full description of the "Mechanisms of Defence" in relation to specific character structures. To interpret at the level of defence mechanisms is not enough. As long as one interprets in terms of fear, frustration, revenge, envy, Oedipus complex, castration anxiety, omnipotent control or whatever, one has not reached the level at which the conflict is rooted. The interpretative task should aim for a more substantial change, which reaches the analysand's occult premises.

Melanie Klein's notion, of unconscious phantasy underlying the transference and accompanying all experience of reality, is suggestive of the idea that there are, in each of us, a series of theories which organize our internal world at an unconscious level. These theories give meaning to our internal objects' interactions (both at a part-object and a whole object level), which in turn find an outlet in the communication to the analyst.

All through Klein's work, the investigation has been into the way in which internal unconscious phantasy penetrates and gives meaning to "actual events" in the external world; and at the same time the external world brings meaning in the form of unconscious phantasies. Yet, her work was still missing a unifying key to this ever-widening understanding, a key that should gather all its complexity and subtlety, thereby giving it a unifying base—a base that could act both as a complete structure and as the meaningful, dynamic, starting point.

I believe that Protoanalysis is just that key to transference and dream interpretation. In fact, Protoanalysis, giving access to the central structure of the person, the hidden root of the individual's psychopathology together with its corresponding defensive strategies, sets the base for all the work to follow, confirming and potentiating the long chain of research begun by Freud and continued to our day.

I would like now to present some clinical material to show how this new understanding has brought about an improvement in the quality of my work, a greater clarity on my part, and a better collaboration on the part of the analysands, with the effect of a speeding up of the analytic process without in any way modifying the basic technique and approach.

VII. CLINICAL CASES

A. KRIS

First, I would like to talk about Kris, a young woman of about 28, who came to me two and a half years ago, encouraged by John, her fiance, who showed her the inconsistency of her behavior and her need for help. In fact, while recognizing that John was the most kind, intelligent and loving man, Kris had developed a sudden inexplicable aversion to him and a desire to betray him, which she promptly proceeded to act out.

Kris is an E-IV of the sexual type[1].

John tried to be patient and understanding, but to no avail. Kris could neither control herself, nor understand her behavior, and soon after she initiated her analysis with me, John left her.

Kris panicked and quickly replaced him with Jim, a fifty-year-old man—rich, married, and with a daughter. After a very brief honeymoon period, the painful calvary began. The analytical process was set in by, and in turn stimulated, the compulsion to repeat her painful early life experiences.

Jim was rich but mean; stingy in every way—with money, and in his capacity to give love. He was also unreliable and prone to suddenly disappear without warning. So, Kris had no assurance of what she could rely on.

To make matters worse, she won her first job position in a forlorn, old hospital establishment, far away from the city where she lived. This was a double blow. Now she was out in the cold in her sentimental life, and far away from Jim and me, from whom at the time she could find the only source of support. So I too became the

---

[1] According to the proto-analysis as taught by Ichazo, each character (according to ruling passion or fixation) comprises three variants, according to the predominance of the sexual, social, or self-preservation drive.

24

mother who was difficult to be reached, who left her alone for long periods, who ignored her pain, her panic, her need.

Kris drank heavily, took self-prescribed tranquillizers and pain-killers, and drove dangerously to and from work (over three hours each way). The only way to continue therapy was to concentrate her three sessions in two days.

A time of anguish and emergency began. Kris was in agony and I feared for her survival. She began to be promiscuous, had a dangerous car accident from speeding and, in the midst of all the upheaval, even had a lesbian experience. In this way Kris was remembering-repeating the painful experiences of her early days: finding again her "memories in feelings," as Klein says, to gain a new understanding of herself and her relation to the world.

Kris is the first child of a deprived, angry mother, who married a weak man for whom she had only contempt. Kris formed a very strong and ambivalent alliance with her mother against the weak men of her family, namely her father and younger brother.

Why had she rejected the kind fiance for the stingy one? And what was to be my role in all this? By the time she came to me, Kris, with her brilliant academic achievements, had reached a sufficient degree of self-respect to be able to begin to look into the abyss of her inner world. At this point in time she needed the following things: to revive the anguish of her past, to have at hand a helper to bear it and understand it with her, to discover that not only should she need not blame herself for it but also that she deserved love and self respect. Finally, she needed to discover that she was not as helpless as she feared. She could take good care of herself, thereby setting her sense of self-esteem on proper foundations.

Up until then Kris's response to pain was sleep, drink, pills, men, lesbian phantasies, and phantasies of some rich older man who would take care of her.

While on the one hand Jim seemed to be the very person who would make her sense of emptiness and her lack of love even greater, paradoxically it was only through such choice that she could see to her deeper needs. In this way, in fact, Kris was compelled to develop a relationship with me that would modify her harsh internal mother into a softer, more loving, and accepting person who would accept her poor masculine image of herself and, at the same time, help her to develop her own capacity to take care of herself and thus deserve her own self-respect and love.

In this context, my function has been to be that softer, more accepting and understanding person who could hold the situation, facilitate its unfolding in a non-judgmental way, bear the anxiety that it caused, and help her in turn to do so. My knowledge of being a type I has enabled me to better check my need for control and judgement, and in this sense, has favored a more accepting attitude towards Kris's chaotic and dangerous behavior. At the same time, the knowledge that she is a type IV has given me a key to interpreting what was happening to her, and a better understanding of her expectations of me, that is, her constant and great fear of my judgement.

In short, the knowledge of her past experience, a clear vision of the interplay of types I and IV in the transference/counter-transference situation, plus a knowledge of her current external life situation understood as externalization of her internal world unconscious phantasies, have enabled me to hold a unitary vision of the person in front of me, to help Kris reconstruct her past in the present with a new, open way to her future.

What comes to my mind at this point is the Sufi tale of "The Elephant in the Dark," which you probably know. An elephant, belonging to a circus, was brought to a small village where no one had ever seen an elephant before. Four curious persons, having heard of the hidden wonder, were impatient to see it immediately and went there straight away. They discovered that the stable was in complete darkness, so they had to carry out their enquiry in the dark.

One of them touched the elephant's trunk and thought that the creature must be like a pipe. A second one touched its ear and thought it was like a fan. The third one, touching a leg, could think of it as a living column. The fourth one put a hand on the elephant's back and was convinced that it was a sort of throne. No one managed to form a complete image, and each of them, in describing what he had perceived, had to use as a point of reference something already known to him.

Confusion was the result of this expedition. Each of them was sure he was right and no one among the village people could understand what had happened—what it was that the four people had actually perceived. (Idries Shah, *The Sufis*, N.Y.: Doubleday, 1964.)

I think this tale explains for me the use of Protoanalysis and the enneatype structure of the personality in relation to psychoanalysis, in the sense that this knowledge confirms all that I have learned with my psychoanalytical training, but, at the same time, it enables me to reach a unitary vision that was missing before.

Coming back to Kris. I had in my mind the picture of the whole elephant while she was gradually discovering its various parts. Thanks to the enneatype structure I could see both the parts and the whole. Knowing where we were has been of tremendous help to me and has favored a more confident and speedy unfolding of the analytical process.

The analytical process, through the relationship with me, has brought about the coming together of Kris's internal family. The brave mother, the protecting father, and the loved daughter have been internally reunited. Thanks to the insight gained through the analysis, Kris has found an interesting external situation to embody this experience. And, interestingly enough, this external event has coincided with a positive transference situation with me and with another very important external event: her return from exile. In fact, she has won a new job application which has brought her back home.

Needless to say, all these events are meaningfully interacting and are the externalization of the internal work accomplished by this young woman.

I shall give you some excerpts from the session in which she brings together all the good feminine figures in her life to repair her mother's image and also gives me an image of her internal reunited family, by playing the good father and indentifying with the nice daughter. This is a very moving session in which she makes a replay of all the important female figures of her life—all the school teachers she has had from primary school to high school—naming all the gifts that the relationship with them brought her.

Then she tells me that she has been dreaming often of me lately. In one dream, in particular, I appear as a mixture of myself and her mother. Kris says: "Yesterday I have seen a photograph of my mother. I felt like crying; I felt we looked alike."

Then she tells me of Mary and Emily. "Mary is a brave woman, who works with handicapped children and lives alone with her little daughter, Emily. I have been invited to their house. They live in a small dream village that seems to be out of time, in an old house, with an old fireplace and an old sink with a marble slab. A house of great poverty and simplicity, yet beautiful. Emily is a very lively child who reminds me of myself as a child. I have already been there two or three times. They are a mother and a child without a man. With them I have felt the spinster aunt, the doctor, the father. Emily has immediately accepted me, and allows me to touch her and to kiss her. She comes into my arms."

* * *

Relevance of the Main Traits Descriptors of Character Structure Number IV to the Understanding of Kris's Psychopathology: (reference throuhout: Claudio Naranjo, *Ennea-type Structures*, Nevada City, CA: Gateways/IDHHB, 1990, pp.67-79.)

Naranjo's descriptions of this type include: chronic sense of inner scarcity and badness because of excessive craving for love; forceful reaching out; intense demand for that which is missed; poor self-concept—prone to shame, feeling ugly, feeling inadequate; connection with vanity—excessive concern with the image of the self and failure to achieve the idealized image.

Kris has always had a bad relationship with her body—critical of her legs in particular—although, in fact, she is a beautiful looking woman. She has had frequent attacks of intense envy of a beautifully sun-tanned model in a dashing swimsuit who was featured on all the billboards of the town. This model was Jim's previous lover. (The envy of the mother here is experienced as envy towards a preferred sibling, as Naranjo observes). We jokingly nicknamed her the "Ocean Model." She was beautiful, but with a hard-looking expression in her eyes: like a perfect marble statue, cold and unapproachable.

Coldness, vindictivness, and hate have been Kris's defences. The atmosphere of turmoil and turbulence, and the tendency to self-victimization and frustration, I have already described. Voraciousness and greediness manifested in her wanting everything immediatly: beautiful house, all comforts, beautiful clothes, expensive car, the best restaurants, etc. Alchool, smoke, drugs. Countersexual identification—underlying lesbianism. She had frequent lesbian phantasies, acted one out on one occasion, and finally managed to sublimate it.

Extreme neediness and the taboo against it—this came up very clearly in a session:

Kris: "It is my mother's fault. She used to tell me to be superior to my brother. 'You are older, you are superior . . .' My mother always gave what she had. She never said no, but then she had an enormous resentment inside. She was full of anger. My mother was very angry with her own father who went bankrupt and, in order to pay the workers, ruined his family, leaving it in great poverty. But then she did the same and took it out on me. She was always angry. She denied being angry with me but I could feel she was. The other big confusion was to ask because you need, and to feel it is bad to do so."

Kris's introjected bad object was a bad mother who hated and despised the father with whom Kris was identified. As Naranjo writes:

> "It is such self-denigration that creates the 'hole' out of which arises the voracity of envy proper in its clinging, demanding, biting, dependent, overattached manifestations." (p. 72)

The Masochistic Traits:

> "...*the use of pain as vindictiveness and an unconscious hope of obtaining love through suffering*..."[which in turn may lead the type IV] "... *to suffer from loneliness and*... *harbor a tragic sense of their life or life in general.*" (p.72)

In Kris's case I would add that she eroticized pain in order to make it more tolerable. On one occasion, during a school test situation in the class, the ever increasing anxiety due to her incapacity to answer the test had culminated in an orgasm.

"Particularly striking is the propensity of the ennea-type IV to the mourning response . . . ." (p. 73): Kris had arranged her life in such a way as to live her inner sense of loneliness, loss, and abandonment to the full every week—with the unreliability of Jim, the long separations from me and Jim, and the long geographical distance from all that was familiar to her.

Emotionality—*"Envious people feel hate intensely* . . ." (p. 75.): Kris remembers how her mouth watered when she beat her brother. Often she wished her lover dead. She burned and destroyed his gifts when angry with him.

Her need to be special and prima-donna was satisfied through her academic brilliance: she always came up first in her course.

The character dynamics as described in the structure of number IV—too much and too little, excessive intensity, the cannibalistic impulse ("Either I eat you or you eat me")— come up very clearly in one session in particular:

Kris: "I have noticed that I am very interested in your plants. I compare them to mine. I think you must like them. Now in my flat I have got two of them. The problem is that the leaves become yellow if I water them too much and also if I do not water them enough. How does one learn to judge the right quantity? I do not know how to do it."

Analyst: "Here together we learn how to get the right measure: that is the way you can learn. In fact, yesterday when you complained about some intervention of mine and I recognized your criticism as valid, you were very surprised and reassured by it. Perhaps as a child you experienced the too much and the too little . . . ."

Kris: "I was obese between the age of one and two. At first my mother gave me only milk and no water, and then I became very fat. That caused my legs to become bent under the excess of weight . . . ."

The corrective experience in the previous session had been my unexpected response to her complaints:

Kris: "Yesterday you confirmed the accuracy of my perceptions. I had feared that you might want to use the logic of your superior analytical knowledge to squash me and prove me wrong, as I would have done had I been in your place. That is why it has taken me a whole week to come out with it. I thought that the admission of having made a mistake would make you go to pieces."

Kris lacked the model of a good relationship in which the one is not dominating the other into submission, but where there is room for both, and reciprocal recognition.

She told me that she had a desire for a very sweet analyst, but had chosen one who had been described to her as strict. One whom you cannot fool.

The other association had been to her not being ready for a loving man like John, thanks to her conviction that you must keep women in their place like Jim does. "Jim holds me in his hand by his behavior that causes me pain, and thinks that this is the right way to behave with women to avoid being manipulated. And I realize that deep down I agree with him. I believe he is right. I cannot really believe that a good relationship can exist."

This shows the vicious circle that feeds hate and destructiveness, of which Strachey speaks. We have broken it to establish a virtuous circle.

This also confirms the character dynamics as described in the structure number IV: Not only, "I am not loved so I am worthless," and "Love me so I know I am all right," but also, "he cannot be worthwhile if he loves me." (See the destruction of the relationship with John.)

Naranjo says:

"These processes are self-frustrating, for love, once obtained, is likely to be invalidated." (p. 79) And further on: *". . . the pursuit of being through the emulation of the self-ideal stands on a basis of self-rejection and of blindness to the value of one's true self (just as the pursuit of the extraordinary involves the denigration of the ordinary). Because of this, ennea-type IV needs, in addition to insight into these traps, and more than any other character, the development of self support that comes, ultimately, from appreciative awareness and the sense of dignity of self and of life in all its forms."* (p. 79)

Kris: "I have the perception of being a rather disturbed person. This is surprising as I don't have a picture of my family, nor of my chilhood, so disturbed as to justify that deep feeling of disturbance that I experience. I feel I am a very disturbed person. Then I feel like saying that it is me, "It is my fault . . . , " and I feel inclined to mistrust my feelings and my judgement as if I had been ill from the very beginning. It is not possible that my parents could be so evil . . . . But then, I cannot trust my perceptions. The alternative is to be ruthless with others . . . ."

Then Kris begins to think more in terms of "self-support": "I fear for my survival. What shall I do? I must make an insurance to prevent the catastrophe that will come. I have no one, I feel alone."

Analyst: "How to account for the apparently contradictory observation that your family was not so bad and yet you felt so rejected and disturbed? Both things are true. Your parents loved you but did not understand your needs and therefore you felt rejected by them. This is the big catastrophe which has already happened in your past and which you fear will repeat in your future."

Kris begins to think about buying a house for herself, but first she wants an insurance on her own person. From situations of deep anxiety and panic comes a turning to ideas of protecting herself. Bit by bit the various aspects of her personality are coming together to make a whole, and Kris is beginning to envision a time when she will be able to take care of herself.

Reconstruction of the Evolution of Kris's Transference:

In one session Kris and I traced back our steps together in the evolution of the transference experience from the very beginning to this day. I reminded her how, at first, she experienced me as the possessive and controlling mother who wanted her for herself and would prevent her from loving the man of her choice. A cruel mother, cruel in her prohibition, but equally cruel if she (the mother) allowed Kris to proceed and hurt herself.

Earlier on still, her use of me had been that of a sounding board to check whether she could trust her own perception of the world that surrounded her. She was afraid of getting mixed up with the beliefs and expectations of her own loved and hated mother. Then, she experienced me as the mother who encouraged her to trust her own feelings and emotions, and to seek the experiences that she felt a need to explore. There was a gradual working through of all this until the various parts came together to form a whole: the reiunification of her inner family.

Kris now can recognize her difficulty in letting go of a tragic vision of herself, where a subtle pleasure and excitment linked to pain still had a hold on her like a drug. This, however, has become much milder and we are beginning to envision a time when she will be able to take good care of herself.

B. JOHN

John is an E-II: Social. This is something I have realized in the course of time, after consultation with Nara Sigward, who is more experienced than I on the enneatype structures.

It is interesting to notice the difference between the two sessions I am going to present: the first, at the beginning of treatment, when I thought that John might belong to the angry type, because of his perfectionism, his intentional goodness, his deep resentment towards his wife, his martyr role and his incapacity to express his aggressiveness; and the second session, more recently, when I shifted my focus from anger to pride, where his basic problem seems to lie.

I have since reconsidered my picture of him in the light of egocentric generosity, which seems to fit better. He is gentle, warm and very charming. He is delighted with himself, and with reason, as he is truly capable, intelligent, creative, highly-educated and sophisticated.

John's aggressiveness is totally repressed; he binds his wife to himself through his giving but, at the same time, his dominance and desire to keep her dependent and infantile make her feel dissatisfied, aggressive, and ever more demanding. This creates a painful and explosive vicious circle. John is totally unable to express his aggressiveness and keep in check that of his wife because of the repression of neediness that the structure of proud character involves.

Typically he has an image of himself as a giver, rather than as a receiver—as Naranjo describes, one filled with satisfation to the point of generous overflowing.

John is unaware of and too proud to show his neediness, and is driven by a compulsion to please and to be extraordinary. Being a gifted person has enabled him, up until now, to uphold this flattering image of himself, but the cracks are showing in his marriage and in his incapacity to cope with the ever increasing demands of his successful business.

Also, in the relationship with me, needless to say, he does all the work, leaving me little space, in fact actively preventing me from making any useful contribution, with his tendency for taking over and conducting the whole thing. At first he had me relegated to the role of the admiring audit. He only wanted my applause and admiration, projecting into me the small needy child and the sense of inadequacy.

I shall report, now, excerpts from two sessions. This first one is at the beginning of treatment and gives the feel of the transference situation:

John: "In these days I am in a state of great anxiety for my work where things are not moving. I realize I spend extra energies through being anxious. I am not satisfied with my office girl, who fails to comply with my instructions. Perhaps it is my fault, because I am unwilling to look for alternatives. I give her general instructions and leave her to get on with it. She is unsure of herself and needs constant guidance. When I could afford to give it, there was no problem, but now I don't have the time to do her work.

The other problem is what I feel when I see others working unsatisfactorily. I am very tempted to say, 'Leave it, I shall do it. I prefer to do it myself.' I had not planned to employ this girl. My wife pressed me into it. Also, circumstances forced me. I was overburdened with work. There were no older and more expert people available. She was young and *tabula rasa*. Perhaps I also preferred it so, as with an older person there would have been the problem of being judged in my way of working."

The analyst drew his attention to his refusal to recognize his need for help.

John: "I would have preferred not to be in the condition of needing it. My wish is for somebody that could do exactly as I would do. The result is that, in my refusal to look for the right collaborator, I chose the first person that turned up. The problem is that, if I have worthwhile collaborators I am no longer "the only one" in the studio. I wanted a person that could be the extension of myself. . . ."

Analyst: "Why such difficulty in finding a true collaborator?"

John: "I cannot trust anybody. I do not want to trust anybody. And yet, in other work situations at present, I am working with colleagues with whom I get on very well. I never wanted colleagues. I always preferred myself, because I want things to be perfect and only I can do it. And when I don't do them perfectly, I become very critical and dissatisfied with myself. If I got help, I am afraid that they would take over and leave me out of things. I do not think I am very good at defending my space and my relationship with others. I am afraid of having to face jealousy, competition, aggressiveness . . . . Perhaps I should engage a young architect to see what the designer-girl cannot do. Somebody that could become a true collaborator and colleague. I realize I see this in a rather negative light, rather than as a positive source of weight-lift for me. I am tempted to say I will do it and not think about it, but then it would be a repetition of the past, like with the office girl designer."

Analyst: "Your first collaborator was chosen as a result of your wife's pressure, and so was your second helper, myself. In fact, you came driven by the fear of losing your wife. Again, you did not choose the analyst to go to, your wife gave you my name. You do not trust your wife and you made no enquiry ahout me. You came compelled by circumstances and without thinking about it, because if you had thought about it you would have refused it.

"You do not want to have to depend on anyone, as deep down you feel you cannot trust anyone, like you did as a child when you decided that your parents were not up to it. This is the way you grew to function now. But this approach is also at the base of your difficulty and stands in the way of your growth."

John: "This is very true. My wife has often complained about my wish to do everything by myself and my lack of trust in her. But, I am pleased with the way our work is proceeding and I feel that it is very important to work on what has come up today."

The second session took place after my recognition that John belonged to enneatype structure II:

John: "I keep having very great difficulties with Jennifer: I am torn between resentment and the need to have a dialogue with her. I am in a muddle between real problems and imaginary ones. I realize I go into a short-circuit, lose contact with reality, and become paralysed. I am enormously angry with Jennifer and I fear that this anger might do irreparable damage."

Analyst: "How could it be destructive to say to Jennifer that you need her? I do not believe this is a problem of anger, rather one of pride."

John: "I do not ask because I cannot bear to be turned down."

Analyst: "The problem could really lie here: you're not presenting yourself as a human being that needs the other person."

John: "I recognize it to be so. This is something which has many stratifications by now. My intolerance of rejection has led me to try and become indispensable. Come to think of it, this is the same as my father did with my mother. I feel I am in a very great confusion. I feel blocked."

Analyst: "To say, 'I need you,' is the natural starting point in a relationship. It is what gives the other his proper space."

John: "I do not want to set aside this way of thinking of mine. But what is the use of this doing all by myself? I have used it as a point of strength, but in fact it is a point of weakness. Already thirteen, fourteen years ago, I realized how absurd this way of proceeding was. I understood it while talking about my relationship problems with two friends. I could feel then that I could not face things because of my pride. At that time too, the problem was a disappointment in love. When I met Jennifer I had a great desire to set aside the long turmoil of my life. My greatest wish was for deep inner peace, but this never happened because I carried on with great inner turmoil.

"I never put my feet on the ground because of a great blotting out. I could not get rid of my previous experience. I could only come to terms with everyday reality, but in a very divided way in relation to Jennifer—this doing everything by myself, a not-knowing how to relate to people. Now I feel very closed. I have no relationships with other people. I have no friends now. Only a memory of friends. Not even with Jennifer I can talk openly. I feel like saying that in these years I have given the worst of myself. I have lost myself. This way of mine has denied the desire that makes for a real and deep relating with people.

"Between giving and taking there must be evenness. It is as if I had lost what constitutes the important input. As if I had wanted to present myself as an adult without actually being one . . . ."

Conclusion:

Without the realization that John belongs to the enneatype II, I would have missed the interplay of denied anger with unconscious neediness, which is crucial to John's risk of losing his wife and destroying his family. In fact, John's denied neediness has meant that he has been projecting his sense of personal insignificance into his wife, Jennifer, who already has a problem of her own on this account. For example, she greatly desired to study and improve herself, but he always obstructed these aspirations of hers, wishing to keep her in a position of dependence.

Furthermore, the extreme inhibition of John's aggressiveness has been an open invitation to unrestrained aggressiveness on the part of Jennifer. This, in turn, has compelled Jennifer to seek help outside the marriage by going into analysis in the first place and, secondly, by starting an extra-marital relationship in the attempt to find alternative ways of growing up.

I believe that the timely recognition of the root of John's pathology might rescue his marriage, which is seriously at risk. Without this greater precision in the reading of his problems, the understanding might have come too late to rescue his relationship.

As a conclusion, this case alerts our attention to three very important considerations:

1) The absolute need to identify the enneatype structure of the analyst and that of the patient, as a pre-requisite to understanding with clarity what happens in the transference.

My initial mistake in the correct identification of John's enneatype structure would have led me in a state of unconscious identification with him, and thereby would have caused me to miss the point of his difficulty. In fact, this is a constant problem in analytical practice: where the analyst may be blinded by his/her counter-transference reaction to the patient. Recognition of the respective enneatype structures can be of invaluable help on this account.

2) The speedy identification of the patient's enneatype structure facilitates the analytical work.

Bearing in mind the main root of the patient's pathology helps the unfolding of the analytical process and favors the coming together of the whole picture, like the elephant of the Sufi tale.

3) This case is a demonstration of how timely recognition of our respective structures may produce insight that might spare this patient the pain of a harder way of getting to know himself, that is, through the loss of his wife and the destruction of his family.

C. GERALDINE

Geraldine is a Type III, Self-Preservation. When I read Naranjo's description of type III—vanity, inauthenticity, and "marketing" orientation—I could get a better measure of Geraldine, who had to learn this in a subtle way for her survival as a young child. In fact, because of a severe condition of illness as a very young child, Geraldine was separated from home and put in an institution. They kept her there for a few years, from the age of two and a half until eight, with a view to giving her better medical care.

Thanks to her unusual intelligence, Geraldine developed a great capacity for impersonating the ideal of the person in front of her. More specifically, her desperate need for security led her to impersonate the utmost ideal of security: the doctor who always has an answer and can reassure everyone, providing the solution to all problems.

Geraldine told me that what kept her alive as a child was her admiration for a doctor, in the institution, who communicated to her the hope of healing through the use of will power. The other source of strength had been her playing the role of the one who could cope, and thus reassure the whole family, and be admired for it. The identification of these two elements— security through impersonation of the ideal of security—has been a very useful key in understanding Geraldine's functioning in life, in the transference, and in the limits that this causes to her growth.

I shall cite two sessions with Geraldine. The first shows how the need for security as a defence operates in the transference with me; the second shows how this need for security has landed Geraldine in an impotent relationship, in which collusively the couple protect each other from facing themselves and reality.

Naranjo says that these people, who usually have difficulty in being alone and in extricating themselves from over-acting achievement, particularly benefit from facing themselves and from bearing the "loss of face" entailed by not looking into the social mirror. This indication has been of great help to me in supporting this patient to face loneliness as a source of potential growth.

As I have said, Geraldine is a type III Self-Preservation: her need for autonomy and search for security are well illustrated by this transcript of a session, which shows her reaction to my informing her that I shall take one week holiday at the beginning of December on top of the usual fortnight holiday for the Christmas break.

Session I

Geraldine: "My brother is ill again. He is very anxious and confused. In order to relieve his anxiety, he buys things trying to avoid customs, and he regularly gets fined. I wonder what kind of customs he is trying to avoid. Dr. X, who is my brother's doctor, has asked me to talk to her about him so I rang her."

Analyst: "Why?"

Geraldine: "It was simply to give her brother, I mean, my brother a sense of being all close around him. I believe he is very frightened of being abnormal.

"Come to think of it, all this does not make a great deal of sense. . . . Every time I stay overnight in Rome, my husband develops some ailment and complains. What a bore! Valery, the head of my department is on holiday in Africa. She had the cheek of demanding that on a specific day we should ring her up in Africa to inform her of how the clinic was faring. I am in charge in her absence and, not only I have refused to do so, but I could not restrain from having a laugh about her with some colleagues on account of this ridiculous request of hers.

"Yesterday, I discovered, from a friend, that my boyfriend had been surprised by my lack of jealousy when he had shown me a photograph of his previous girlfriend."

Analyst: "Your brother is trying to avoid facing himself in this moment of difficulty, like you do now with me, with regard to my leaving you in December. But, as you say, it does not pay in the end.

"Every time I leave you, you defend yourself from feeling alone or insecure by becoming the one who reassures everybody else. You swap places with your brother's doctor. She becomes his sister in need of reassurance. It is I who shall be anxious about how you will fare during my absence, and it is I who will want to have your news, like Valery, your Head of Department. And, finally, I shall be jealous of the person you will be with during my absence, while you will be quite calm."

Session II

This second session shows how, in not facing her feelings about the imminent separation from me, Geraldine can only act them out, with the implications of risking to remain trapped into eternal repetition by her defence strategies.

Geraldine: "I had a dream: My brother was in a therapeutic community. They were telling me that things were not going well. My brother comes to see me and I get the impression that things are going better than what they have been saying, and there is talk of him re-entering the therapeutic community."

Then, Geraldine told me of her heroic effort to spend an evening on her own at her *pied-a-terre* in Rome, but instead, she gave in to the wish to visit a very nice colleague and his wife. This couple was very warm and welcoming, and persuaded her to eat with them and sleep at their place.

She told me further that, on the previous day to our appointment, she had a very long and intense discussion with her husband. They told each other a lot of unpleasant true things, that might imply a need to separate. For the first time in years, Geraldine was able to tell him that she did not want to continue an impotent relationship, in which he did not contribute either sex or money. He told her in return that he needed a little more time to sort himself out, but he would not stand in her way if she wanted her freedom.

The surprising upshot of this was that Geraldine decided she would look for a new house for them both, near her place of work.

Finally Geraldine told me that she has had meetings with heads of therapeutic communities, where she has been strenuously defending the case of a young man who is no longer a drug-addict, but who needs day-care and therapy sessions with her to prevent relapse. The heads of the therapeutic communities were not pleased. They had asked the boy to choose between staying in the community for a period of four years and the treatment suggested by Geraldine. The boy had chosen Geraldine's treatment.

Analyst: "Your reaction to my leaving you alone for nearly a month is that you are not well and that you must go back to the therapeutic community represented by the relationship with your husband, and that is the reason why you have suddenly decided that you must look for a house for the two of you, in contrast with your recent thinking.

"However, you are not as ill as all that, and you could manage quite well out of that therapeutic community which does not foster the growth of either of you, as you rightly realized during your discussion with your husband. This, ultimatly, is the same type of help that you are trying to give to your patient—to help him face himself and his life out in the world."

Geraldine: "I see. This explains why this sudden urge to get a house, and also the passionate way in which I fought to keep this young man out of the community and give him a chance. It also explains why I have been paying for my husband all these years. It made me feel grown up."

Analyst: "That young man you are trying to keep out of the community is also your chance to be free with my support."

Comments:

I think Geraldine is a very tricky patient, because of her fear of letting go of her defences. She requires a firm hand and a keen eye. The knowledge of her strategies and defences is of tremendous value in my being able to make sense of her often ambiguous comunications.

REFERENCES

1. Etchegoyen, R.H., *The Fundamentals of Psychoanalitic Technique,* London: H. Karnac Books Ltd., 1991.

2. Freud, A. (1936), *The Ego and the Mechanisms of Defence,* in: *Collected Writings,* Vol. 2, 1965-71.

3. Freud, S. (1910 a), *Five Lectures On Psychoanalysis,* S.E. 11; (1912 b) *The Dynamics of Transference,* S.E. 12; (1920 g) *Beyond The Pleasure Principle,* S.E. 18, London: The Hogarth Press.

4) Greenson, R.R. (1967), *The Technique and Practice of Psychoanalysis,* London: Hogarth Press, volume 1.

5) Isaacs, S. (1943), "The Nature and Function of Phantasy," *International Journal of Psychoanalysis* 29 (1948) pp. 73-97.

6. Klein, M. (1952 a), "The Origins of Transference" in: *Writings,* Vol. 3, "Envy and Gratitude and Other Works" (Chap. 4), 1975.

7. Kris, E. (1951), "Ego Psychology and Interpretation In Psychoanalytic Therapy," *Psychoanalitic Quarterly* 20: 15-30.

8. Lacan, J. (1964), *The Four Fundamental Concepts of Psycho-Analysis,* Cambridge University Press, 1988.

9. Meltzer, D. (1978), *The Kleinian Development,* vol. 1-3, Perthshire, Scotland: Clunie Press.

10. Meltzer, D. (1981), "The Kleinian Expansion of Freud's Metapsychology," *International Journal of Psychoanalysis* 62: 177-185.

11. Naranjo, C. (1990), *Enneatype Structures,* Nevada City, CA: Gateways, IDHHB Inc.

12. Reich, W. (1933) *Character Analysis,* New York: Orgone Institute Press, 1945

13. Strachey, J. (1934), "The Nature of the Therapeutic Action of Psychoanalysis," *International Journal of Psychoanalysis,* 15: 127-159.

14. Thomae H. & Kaechele H. (1985), *Psychoanalytic Practice,* Berlin: Springer-Verlag; *Trattato Di Terapia Psicoanalitica,* Bollati Boringhieri, 1990.

Chapter 3

ENNEATYPES IN THE HOFFMAN QUADRINITY PROCESS (FORMERLY FISCHER-HOFFMAN PROCESS)

by SUZANA STROKE

I. Introduction

I have worked as a psychotherapist using the Fischer-Hoffman method (or Quadrinity Process) since 1978. Until 1986 I applied the method over thirteen weeks in group and individual format; that is, each patient participated in group sessions and also received individual sessions with one of the therapists assigned to him or her during the therapy. From the end of 1986 to this date I have worked with the intensive one-week format, in which the patient's participation focuses more on group sessions and the specific therapist intervenes in each case according to the needs that emerge, without any anticipated determination. Furthermore, within this format there are also situations with small groups in which more individualized work is possible. I was directly or indirectly in charge of nearly 2,000 patients during these 15 years of practice.

Since the Enneagram of personalities became known to me in 1987, with Claudio Naranjo's arrival in Belo Horizonte and my involvement with his teaching, my own personal life has been greatly affected, and simultaneously, in a spontaneous way, my professional practice has changed dramatically. The possibility of being able to diagnose, very quickly, my patients' characters (together with the interaction with the therapeutic staff who also took part in the personal work with Claudio) allowed me to go into the therapy in much greater depth and to carry out my work far more efficiently.

Looking back, I can now reach certain conclusions with regard to enneatypes in the Hoffman Quadrinity Process. As many people know, the Process is a directive therapy with cathartic emphasis focusing on the emotional aspect, with little room for intellectualization, and few concepts. It strongly stresses spirituality as well as bodywork (this aiming mainly at emotional expression and recognition of physical blocking).

My intention here is to develop what happens to the ego of each enneatype in a therapy with the characteristics mentioned above. (The word "ego" meaning character, or everything that can be defined as the human machine, the human being's automatism, the conditioning that separates him from his essence.)

I have observed that, depending on each enneatype's more or less deeply rooted tendencies, there is a need for more specific action on the therapist's part (independent of the basic orientation of the method resorted to) in order to obtain results leading beyond the symptoms presented or the explicit needs shown by the client. In general, the client begins to work with her most frequent and obvious character traits, which are rarely relevant to the central nucleus of her character, since, as is generally the case, the ego defends itself constantly, and the person's most immediate desire is merely to escape from pain, from discomfort, and to return to or keep up the status quo with simply a little more control over her own mechanisms. Obviously, this type of situation is variable depending upon the level from which the person starts working.

Starting from my knowledge of the Enneagram, my vision of therapy changed a great deal, mainly my interest in results. The Quadrinity Process as a structure aims at focusing on the origins (in childhood) of the client's conditionings, and helping him to connect with their consequences in adult life, so that, after shedding light on his compulsions, he can commence a continuous process of self-observation and effective change in the different areas of his life. In the first years of my practice, with the training I had received and the experience I gradually acquired, I worked mainly with a very direct and indiscriminate confrontation with the character traits that were apparent in the client—a considerably strong demand in terms of acceptance of working proposals. The emotional expression corresponding to each phase was considered to be the breakdown of resistance, and consequently the opening to a new level of awareness. There was very little tolerance for different levels of capacity, rhythm, or simply the person's individual moment.

With time, and having understood how each enneatype operates with its different forms of resistance, as well as the different expressions of a "liberating experience" as opposed to what I went on to call "ego inflation," the results turned out to be the most important objective of my work (naturally with a whole variety of greater or lesser levels according to what was individually possible within the working proposal).

Therapy can appear to be successful both in the eyes of the therapist and those of the patient, but often it can be merely the ego's success, and vice versa; therapies that apparently are failures can have the best results.

What I have observed to be the most successful cases are those in which the ego loses its hold over the person's life (the most central features become conscious and are under control), and the person carries on with the work on herself and begins some kind of spiritual journey. That is, she is aware that she needs to continue this work on herself, that the road is long and constant, that she needs to pay a great deal of attention to the question of perceiving the more subtle aspects of her ego with a correct intention in her decisions, and coherent action in her behavioral changes. The need for a spiritual guide and the support of therapeutically-oriented groups of a continuous or sporadic nature become the person's own choice and responsibility.

Obviously, the cases with the least success have been those in which the person leaves the therapy with an inflated ego. This situation can reveal too much autonomy, together with the compulsive desire to guide others and "know it all" (more typically in enneatypes II, III and VIII), or on the contrary, a pathological dependence, experienced as unconditional surrender (more frequent in enneatypes IV and VI).

Between these extremes I have also had the chance to observe results that I consider to be therapeutic failures, but not as serious as those of self-deception mentioned above. Instead, these cases are of people who achieve merely a temporary relief from their problems, due to the fact that they do not confront the consequences of their conditioning, but only the causes. They see the features that have hurt them in their childhood. They express their anger, their hatred, their pain. But, they are not capable of recognizing these features in themselves, and, as an immediate consequence, are incapable of forgiving and of experiencing compassion and love. Or instead, they experience these feelings simply because they are present in the therapeutic situation and can use the group's energy, but lack their own profound surrender and awareness. I consider these cases to be less serious than those of ego inflation because the person will shortly have to return to some kind of therapeutic assistance since he has no control over his situation, and his problems lead him to suffer again, or to suffer for the first time (as can be the case for those who come to the Process with very little awareness of having any kind of problem in their lives).

From a statistical point of view I considered that 50% of the cases I encountered were successful, 30% were intermediate cases, and 20% were failures. I considered these cases beyond the duration of the therapy itself, since in general the results are revealed some months after the therapy, and sometimes even one or two years later.

With regard to what I mentioned above, about my change of therapeutic focus as a consequence of my discovery of the Enneagram, the successful results increased considerably in comparison to previous results.

II. Participation Statistics

The great majority of patients participating in the Hoffman Quadrinity Process in Belo Horizonte belonged to enneatypes IV and VI—nearly 60%. They are followed by types V, II and III—an average 30%. There is a frequency of approximately 10% of types I, VII and IX. As is already well-known, type VIII is the most unusual person in the therapeutic environment. In my experience I can say that there has been a participation of 1%.

III. The Effects Of The Therapy On The Different Enneatypes

Enneatype I

This type of person generally comes because of problems in the relationship with the partner. His or her aim is to change their partner, to find a way to control the conflictive situation, to establish rules and commitments; they hardly ever come to the Process because of their own need.

Since the Quadrinity Process is a very confrontative method and there is not much time for chatting or indulgence, type I will quickly accept the rules of the game if the staff and the individual therapist take on a reliable and sufficiently capable authority, responding to type I's obedience with an assertiveness and knowledge that allows the client to go ahead with the therapy without hesitation.

The tasks of the type I are carried out with discipline. They speak with considerable honesty, and have an intellectual knowledge of their problems. Body and emotional expression are very poor, but the therapeutic stimulus in the cathartic sessions allows them to break down the barriers preventing emotional contact.

Experience of essence or the spiritual being—a very powerful and constant characteristic of the Hoffman Quadrinity Process—is generally very new and important for type I. They have considerable difficulty in surrendering themselves, due to their mental rigidity, but, on the other hand, they make use of their intense desire for finding virtue, and this is an aid to opening up on a deeper level.

The final result of the therapy is quite positive. The ego is shaken and weakened, values are greatly questioned, and the person is highly motivated to continue with his search for new elements, mainly in the body and spiritual areas, besides greater freedom in his emotional expressiveness.

Enneatype II

These people come to the Hoffman Quadrinity Process as a result of the suggestions from their partners or family. Their attitude is that of a person without problems, but one who feels curiosity and the desire to know why the person who provided them with the incentive insisted so much on their going. In many cases they need to know what happened to their partner when the partner experienced the Hoffman Quadrinity Process in order that they (the type II) may continue manipulating and using their previous schemes. In other cases they are motivated by the therapy's brief and definite duration. In some cases the challenge of a therapy that is known to be difficult and with something mysterious to it is the main motivation.

The game of seduction is something that appears almost immediately, as well as the need to be the center of attention. Confrontation before the group causes great resistance; humiliation provokes immediate resentment. The therapist has to take on a serious, self-confident authority, with moments of gentleness. This enneatype plays games all the time, coming out of one game in order to start another one, and their need for turning the therapeutic relationship and the group into their object of manipulation competes greatly with their need for working on themselves. This is a person who needs a therapist with a high level of attention who can constantly point out the direction to be followed.

Lack of discipline and difficulty in keeping to commitments are also character traits of enneatype II that contribute to the confrontation of their real participation, since commitments are required as regards punctuality in the group and written tasks.

The type II's facility for emotional expression can often be merely a way of using therapy in order to be "the best," especially when the method focuses on emotional and body expression. This greater ease with emotional contact can be directed towards primitive nuclei of conditioning as well as towards spirituality in the induced meditations, which can, in many cases, lead the individual to deeper and more important discoveries, stimulating her to fight her conditioning and resistances.

We can say that, in general, results with enneatype II are superficial, with few cases of therapeutic success. In many cases, the ego takes over the success and the individual leaves the therapy with a considerable inflation: feeling that she is the most capable, most brilliant person, with the greatest rights to do what she pleases; justifying herself in each act; exploiting the knowledge she has acquired; masking the shortcomings through an emphasis on the defects of others. For example, after the Process, a woman belonging to type II decided to separate from her husband. Feeling strong, the mistress of her life, she demanded—resorting to the law—that he quit the house, leaving their child as well as their car with her, and charging him the highest alimony she could manage to get. She felt she had the right to this because she had made contact with her capacity for living alone, without depending on her husband, and since she had suffered in their unsatisfactory relationship, without being able to make the decision to leave him. But now, after having felt some of her real possibilities, she does not perceive the selfishness ruling her, nor that he is not the only one to blame for her dissatisfaction.

In order to overcome the ego, or go into their development in greater depth, these type II people need to make a considerable effort, and also acquire a humility that will allow them to make a correct usage of the temporary power and well-being they have achieved.

Enneatype III

This type of person generally comes to the Process because it is fashionable, or due to the quickness of the therapy, or because of frustrations in love. They adapt quite well to the method, and are organized, disciplined, obeying the strict rules as long as they can admire at least one of the therapists on the staff. They quickly try to be "the top of the class," and devote their energy to "doing well." They attempt to understand the mechanism of the method and produce the results they imagine to be the ones expected. They have great difficulty in expressing their emotions, play-acting rather than genuinely showing their emotions. Spirituality is generally rejected as something abstract which they cannot control. Owing to their need to stand out and to finish what they have begun, they make great efforts.

In general, type III's manage to overcome their emotional blocking, making contact with an unknown world which provides them with great satisfaction and a considerable surrender to the method. The experiences that take place appear to catch them by surprise, and their dedication and effort start to work in favor of their development. In some cases, when the ego is very strong, and the blocking is very structured, superficiality is kept up, and results are superficial too. When there is real success, the danger lies in the inflation of the ego, which here also very easily takes over the individual's achievements. In these situations, the vanity of having been able to break down barriers leads the person to feel better than the rest, and to run the life of others according to his new reference points.

Enneatype IV

This enneatype is one of the most frequent participants in the Process. These are people who enter very easily into the work. They have a gift for expressing their emotions and feel a great need for attention and care. When they sense that they are in an environment that reminds them of what they have always felt, they try to take up all the space in order to talk endlessly about this. Their pain and suffering fit in with the first part of the Process, but when the time comes to leave their attachment to the past and their pain behind and to look for something to live for, these enneatype III's generally come up with all kinds of games for staying where they are. Suffering is their reason for living, and the facts justify their premise to perfection so that they do not want to let go of anything. It is very difficult to get them to make the step to come to the end of the therapy. There are moments of profound connection, of very beautiful experiences, but any little thing takes them back to their habitual way of life.

Most people belonging to this type reach the end with many discoveries, understanding themselves much more, even laughing at themselves, but they have to keep their eyes open with regard to their ingrained, central idea that to get anywhere they always have to suffer. They also have to overcome their transference with the therapist, which easily turns into dependence.

Enneatype V

These are people in need of special attention and great care in contact, mainly in direct confrontation however mild it may be. (Even a remark like, "Speak up," can be very counterproductive.) These people easily disappear in the group, and since they are very observant, if they do not find evidence of having been seen and understood, they tend to disconnect and to lose interest, invalidating their work and the method. The presence of a therapist who is sensitive and intellectually very capable (for this is the area the type V's rely on) is important in order to break down the barrier of distrust, thus proving to the person that her therapist knows more about her than she herself does, or can at least see what the individual has always known about herself but was never able to express.

The enneatype V's have great difficulty not only in expressing any kind of emotion, but also simply in speaking clearly about their experiences in life. Being in a group is a great challenge for enneatype V. They feel threatened and prefer always to solve their problems on their own, or simply to give up and stay as they are. Since the Process requires a great deal of expression, it is necessary for the therapist to keep these difficulties in mind, helping the person individually by making her understand her problems intellectually, to begin with, and then touching her sensitivity (which is great, but almost unattainable) and her pain (nearly entirely forgotten). Furthermore, it is convenient for the therapist to resort, although with great tact, to physical contact (something which this type has always shunned) in order to make the person aware of her usual state of aridity and lack of feeling.

For this type of person the Process can be very efficient, and even lead to great transformations, providing her with a new vision of life and of her possibilities, besides a broader and more persistent continuity in her search. Discovery of the emotional world allows these people to open up communication with the outside world and with affective relations, without having to go through an intellectual filter. Their spiritual experiences are highly stimulating and motivating.

Enneatype VI

These are also people who make quite good use of the Process. They come to it with a great deal of mental confusion, with an intellect full of information and rationalized experiences that considerably magnify the doubts and insecurities typical of this character. As soon as they are able to begin to trust the staff and understand how simple it is to go into their childhood experience, without having to find complicated answers to their difficulties or existential problems, type VI can experience the importance of relying on their own emotions and experiences, without fearing them, turning them into monsters, or projecting them onto others as a defense.

They have considerable difficulty in adapting to the rhythm of the Process, and they also need to be confronted with quite a lot of severity and self-confidence, together with affection and understanding. Over and over again they attempt to prove that they know more or need something different from the needs of the other members of the group. But, once they are able to taste the benefits of trusting the method, they increasingly open up and surrender themselves to it.

In general, the greatest danger with this enneatype, when they are successful, is their fanaticism and their idolatry. They can turn the method and the therapists into something far beyond what they really are, just as these type VI's can also partake in megalomaniacal trips. Another tendency is the dependence they try to maintain with their therapist on the basis of games such as "I can't find solutions to my problems on my own," or "I need the guidance or approval of somebody greater than me." These are people who like to stay in therapy for the rest of their lives. In this sense, the Process confronts them with these false beliefs. They can benefit greatly from their work if they are made to rescue their own core, trust it, and begin to live centered in it.

Enneatype VII

Few people belonging to this type come to the Process, mainly because it is a well-known fact that the method focuses very harshly on childhood pain, and enneatype VII shuns this kind of confrontation. When they come they do so with only a lukewarm involvement, motivated generally out of curiosity, in order to broaden their knowledge, to know what others know.

They have enormous difficulty in accepting the authoritarian manner employed by the Process. They try to challenge the staff intellectually, or establish alliances with group members in order to discredit the therapists. They do this by resorting to their sense of humor, acting as the clowns of the group, or by diverting people's attention from their work. It is necessary to unmask their games in an intelligent, shrewd way, quickly opening their deepest wounds, so that they can concentrate on themselves, changing the importance of their verbal expressiveness into emotional expressiveness.

They are greatly attracted by experiences on a spiritual level, and they have a tendency to exaggerate what they experience. It is very important not to leave them in their deception, even though this might cause frustration and the possibility of invalidating the work they are doing. It is necessary to be constantly on guard in order to bring them down to earth, to make them be specific about what they are experiencing, and observant of the working discipline.

If these difficulties are overcome they can achieve excellent, far-reaching results, changing their lives greatly.

Enneatype VIII

These people are the least frequent in the Process, for reasons that by now are rather obvious. When they come they have no difficulty in entering into the first phase, in which the most primary emotions are worked on. But, they also have a lot of problems with authority, and it is necessary to impose an authority that is more intellectual than forcible. They reject gentleness and see it as a trap. They are quite seductive and try to pick out defects in the staff, while allowing themselves to show a better authority, thus taking over the group. It is necessary to keep a very tight rein on this enneatype, without any allowances. Initial contact is essential in order to determine who is the authority, not only when it comes to running the method, but also, and most important, in the perception and knowledge of the character of this type of individual. If he is made to feel that he is in reliable hands he will open up quite easily in the first phase of the Process—expressing rage, revenge, rejection, etc., with considerable authenticity. In general, they have a clear idea of what made them rebel in their childhood, and, since they have experienced this quite intensely (without repression) throughout their lives, they have no difficulty in doing so now with regard to their parents (apart from the fact that this is precisely something they have always wanted to do). But, they do experience difficulties in understanding the difference between action and reaction, in understanding that they are merely living in their parents' shadows, without making any decisions of their own.

They also experience great difficulty in expressing pain, gentleness, mildness, and they reject spirituality considerably, because they want concrete things. When the second phase of the

Process is reached they try to escape in order not to experience compassion. They are very much afraid of becoming weak. When they manage to complete this phase correctly, great changes take place. They become people with an enormous potential for effecting great changes in their lives, opening up to the search for something more profound, and making use of their tendency for seeking justice in a more compassionate manner, and at the service of a greater power. However, there is also the possibility of their ego taking over. They can easily come out of the Process feeling more in possession of truth, with the desire to put the world and people to rights, singlehandedly. In these cases they can deceive themselves with their self-perception. Since they feel more sensitive, less aggressive, more compassionate, more understanding, and with a greater capacity for empathy, they can use this new way of relating and being in the world to feel that they have even greater rights over people, imposing their "truths" on others and hence leaving their own egoic nuclei untouched.

Enneatype IX

These people do not generally come to the Process due to a decision of their own. Instead, they are generally brought by someone else—their partner, friends, or relatives. They do not feel the need for therapy and do not know where to start working on themselves, having made very few demands on life since childhood. Their tendency is to accept things as they were and are. There is no vibration of *life*, only doing what they think *must be done*. They are quite good at obeying and following the established rules. Sometimes they are brought to the Process by some great pain related to a separation, by frustrations at work, or by serious problems with rebellious children.

Type IX's follow the method quite well as far as external instructions are concerned. They keep their commitments, participating in the group, but experience great difficulties in the first accusatory phase of the Process when they have to look their parents and their childhood in the face and adopt a strong position with regard to what really happened. They tend to resort to distractive mechanisms—falling asleep at moments of deeper experiences, laughing when others cry, asking silly questions in order to remove tension, writing pages and pages about irrelevant matters.

They need strong confrontations that can touch on their dignity, making them blow up and react emotionally. Sometimes even physical pain becomes necessary, as for instance, physical exhaustion. Their tendency to mingle with the group is a help in this case. They can be infected with the group's energy, letting go without having a clear idea of their own motivation, and thus being able to take advantage of the immediate results, without trying to elaborate them until afterwards. In many cases there are quite strong regressions, and it is necessary to lead type IX's by the hand, explaining with great simplicity what is happening to them so that they can integrate it little by little. When they manage to get in touch with their spiritual essence they initially feel frightened, but they can immediately put this discovery to good use and follow up on it.

The next phase of the Process is generally easier for them, but also quite subtle. Rather than truly experiencing compassion leading to the severance of the paternal and maternal link, they can easily enter into the pain produced by their separation from their parents owing to their tendency to symbiosis. It is important to keep a close watch on their progress from the second part of the Process to the end so that they can keep on strengthening their contact with themselves and find a motivation of their own to carry on. Their jovial and friendly expressions can easily be confused with the expressions of a more genuine joy originated through the liberation from conditioning and the expansion of the person's inner world.

In general, results with this enneatype are excellent. They leave the Process with greater liveliness and a far broader perception of themselves and the things around them, but they need a great deal of stimulus in order to stay in touch and keep on working. The tendency to conform leads them to return to their usual routine in the belief that they will be able to maintain their achievements without having to engage in further efforts.

Chapter 4

THE MEETING OF ENNEATYPES IN THE THERAPEUTIC RELATION —A ROUND TABLE—

with Antonio Pacheco, Riccardo Zerbetto, Suzana Stroke, Agueda Segado, Annie Chevreaux, Ignacio Lopez, Joan Garriga, Laura Martinez, Elena Revenga, and Paco Peñarrubia (former president of the Spanish Gestalt Association), Chairman.

Claudio Naranjo: It is natural for us to have scheduled this discussion immediately after the one on forms of transference, since the matter of transference is somewhat simpler. The therapeutic relationship implies a transferential aspect, but it also has a counter-transferential side. It implies a mutual relationship between two people. And, besides the fact that there is always a style of relationship contributed by each, there is something that goes beyond the mere aggregate of these two styles. The encounter between transference and counter-transference is a particular form of relation, and certain relations are easier, whereas others are more difficult. In everyday life we say that two people are compatible, or that they are not compatible. But, the question gets more complicated due to the fact that the most difficult relationships are not necessarily the worst, since they generally involve a very special potential.

The idea for this discussion crystallized after a conversation I had with Riccardo Zerbetto. During a visit to Italy some months ago, I spoke to Riccardo about what he would like to do in the Symposium. He spoke to me of his difficulty (as type II) in his therapies with patients belonging to this same type, and how in these cases a situation arose that was very difficult for him, but also worthwhile. He knew that if this difficulty could be overcome it was something worth tackling.

As I listened to Riccardo it seemed to me that what he had to tell about his experience deserved a detailed explanation. I was sure that this must also be the case for others, and we have often spoken about this when talking about the characters in general in our workshops: How sometimes it is therapeutic, for example, for type I to be near type VII in order to bring the type I out of his/her excessive seriousness with a little playfulness. (The same can be said of all the complementing characters.) Our subject now is the same, only in the professional relationship.

The relevance of the encounter between certain characters during the course of psychotherapy is a subject that is acquiring current relevance. Sufficient attention is beginning to be paid to the fact that the relationship between certain characters can be, in itself, therapeutic.

I would not like this discussion to end without giving consideration to which encounters between characters seem to be a gift in themselves, due to enrichment because of complementary qualities, or because one understands the other well, or whatever.

There are therapists who enjoy therapy with people of their own enneatype. After having learned so much about helping themselves and discovering so many things about themselves, they have acquired a capacity for understanding the patient. At other times this enjoyment is a factor of certain complementary qualities that

can be seen in the Enneagram, qualities which appear to be especially favorable.

I refer to this matter in detail so that it is not neglected or
eclipsed by the other general issue, which is more on the qualita-
tive side: that of the particular qualities of each of the possible
types of relationships between enneatypes.

Paco Peñarrubia: We are going to begin this discussion.
There is a therapist here representing each enneatype. I imagine
you already know them. As a type I therapist we have Antonio
Pacheco, from Vitoria; as type II we have Riccardo Zerbetto, from
Italy; as type III, Suzy, from Brazil; as type IV, Agueda Segado,
from Madrid; as type V, Annie Chevreaux, from Madrid; as type
VI, Ignacio Lopez, who works here in Alicante; as type VII, Joan
Garriga, from Barcelona; as type VIII, Laura, from Menorca; and
as type IX, Elena Revenga, from Alicante.

Our idea is to begin with a brief run-through, for each participant to describe how he or she feels when it comes to acting as a
therapist. In what sense does he or she see that he or she has such
and such resources, or such and such difficulties? We shall not be
speaking specifically in this first round about any of the characters,
but only sharing the point of view of the character of the person
speaking.

Antonio Pacheco: The first thing I do, as a preservation type
I, when I begin to work, is worry. I think it is a principle of excessive concern for the person. I sometimes adopt a fatherly attitude
which, in principle, can help favor the transference, although it is
different for each type.

I worry about all the aspects of the therapy. I worry about being specific, about everything being clear. I worry about doing it
well, about making good use of the time. I do not feel content if at
the end of a session the person has not reaped some kind of benefit; that is, if he or she has not become aware of something, has
not solved some problem, or reached some interesting conclusion.
That is where I feel frustrated, and my concern is doubled, and I
resolve to improve for the next session. Perhaps it is fear of failing,
of not doing well, and, as a consequence, a fear of receiving nega-

tive transference.

This situation has gradually become more relaxed in the last few years, with practice and experience. Nonetheless, I believe that it is quite an influential aspect in the relationship, leading me sometimes to be tense and to channel the work in excess, whereby I miss out on certain things. But, it gradually decreases as the relationship becomes deeper.

I believe that one positive quality would be my willingness to become involved in the relationship with each person, and one difficulty is that my concern can derive into demands made on the person.

Riccardo Zerbetto: I would like to know if statistically enneatype II is more highly represented than other types as far as therapists are concerned. I hope not, because there is a tendency in type II to take charge of others' conditions of weakness—to take charge of children or weak people—since there is a defense of their own dependent weakness. Type II's exemplify this business of projecting onto others what is missing, of occupying a position of power and help, the typical position of the therapist.

In order to become a therapist training is necessary, and type II have difficulty in being trained because they have difficulty in accepting authority–granting somebody else the capacity to help them, and the superior knowledge to grant them recognition.

This need to be recognized, that is so strong, also involves a vulnerability, a susceptibility. These are therapists who do a great many things, who learn many techniques, but type II do not frequently follow a complete personal therapeutic process. They generally deal with incurable situations which normal therapists cannot handle. Type II devote themselves to curing the incurable: psychotics, drug addicts, anorexia nervosa . . . . And a lot of them work with families, because there is a strong sense of control, rather than of the intimacy of the given situation.

Suzy Stroke: What helps me is self-confidence. I feel that others see me as somebody self-confident, and that helps a lot at first. The ease with which I can impose authority with understanding also contributes, whereby a relationship of trust is quickly created in most cases.

The greatest difficulty is when there is a confrontation directed toward myself. Even when the confrontation is not clear, not explicit, still this unsettles me a lot. My immediate reaction (this was more frequent before, although I feel that it still exists) is to become aggressive and assert myself in an authoritarian way. At that moment the relationship does not flow so much. I have to get back to myself, to calm down, to understand what is happening to me. This weakness in confrontation, the difficulty in receiving any kind of criticism is very difficult for me, and the compulsion to react aggressively is something I am constantly working on.

Agueda Segado: I have been reflecting on how I deal with my patients, and it has to do with my stock of knowledge: my background, character, training in Gestalt, and personal evolution. As far as character is concerned, I am a self-preservation type IV.[1] The most significant features of this type when it comes to working are:

Tenacity: I am tenacious when the patient has difficulties, resistances, etc. I try one way or another. I pursue the issue until the person comes round—that is, surrenders him or herself to experience. When that happens I am totally *with* the person. It is hard, but I feel that the effort is worthwhile, both for the patient and for me.

Tenacity in its positive aspect helps the patient work, but it is negative when the patient persecutes him or herself, and above all in particular moments of the process in which you have to slacken off so the person can take on his/her own responsibilities.

Perceiving what is missing: Due to my enneatype, I have a great ability for knowing what is *not* taking place, what remains to be brought out . . . . In what way is this beneficial? The person discovers his/her dark side and integrates it in his/her personality, with the resulting strength this integration involves. What would be the difficulty? Sometimes I do not value what has already been achieved, and I am more aware of what is missing.

---

[1] According to the proto-analysis taught by Ichazo, each character (according to ruling passion or fixation) comprises three variants according to the predominance of the sexual, social, or self-preservation drive.

Introjection: I find it easy to know where others are heading for because I identify with them. But another risk for me is that I can become a garbage can.

The basic thing is that since I am familiar with pain I can lead others easily to enter into profound processes and breakdown. I offer them trust and calm. I am not afraid of what they may find or what they may go through.

My training and personal evolution: These have been highly significant when it comes to being with my patients. I can say that I have gone from a rigid and tenacious attitude to a more compassionate and loving attitude embracing the entire person. For me, the most important thing is no longer personality but the essential part of the person.

I have also observed that, either by coincidence or as a result of contagion, my patients have gradually gone through the same issues and subjects that I have encountered throughout my process. I have not been able to accompany any patient beyond the places I myself have reached.

Annie Chevreaux: I believe I help people with tolerance. I feel I can listen to everything. I am not confused by any issue, and I think this makes the relationship easier.

I also help my patients a lot to remove their guilt, to do what they want to do, to dare to make mistakes and, above all, to realize how they are exploited by their environment or how they let themselves be exploited and how they miss out on the things they want to do. I insist on them being as specific as possible about what they are talking. I do not let them speak in a general manner. I help them focus their awareness on very specific things. That is, they talk to me about their life, not about abstractions.

My limitation, although this is something that is gradually improving as time goes by, is my phobia of falsehood. At the beginning I would get paranoid, especially with type III, because I experienced the falsehood of type III as rudeness. I would say, "They think I'm stupid, they don't trust me, they are lying to me." I found it difficult to understand that this was their problem, that they were not attacking me, and I felt very inadequate for working with this character type.

Now things are changing. I accept others' falseness more, and I accept people talking in general, after having realized the excessive persecution I was exercising. Nevertheless, I think that after the fourth session people know what's going on. They already know the culture, how we are going to work and that I am not going to let them wander off from the subject, because I can't work like that. Some have left, but have then come back after two or three months really wanting to work.

Ignacio Lopez: I'm going to talk a little about my attitude when working, when I am sitting before a patient. This also has to do with my training. I never consider the possibility that I am going to have a new patient. When they call me, or I know somebody is going to come, I don't stop to think about it because that is when I would go into the fact that it scares me. "What will happen...?" I don't do that. I simply sit there in front of the patient. I sit in front of him or her in a very open, very attentive way, not so much with regard to what he/she is telling me, although that too, but to what effect he/she has on me. The patient can make me feel afraid because suddenly I see my father in front of me, or because he or she can seduce me. But, that is how I get an idea of what the other person is like, starting from how I react.

Contrary to Suzy, I think I work very well with doubt. I use doubt to doubt what the patients are telling me with such confidence. That is my way of working, above all with the more confident enneatypes.

Then, I think I'm very flexible. I work a lot with humor and irony, but in a rather benevolent manner. I feel that I want to help people to the extent of my capacity, and I think this allows them to trust me too.

I can always get stuck in intellectual junk. Suddenly I realize that I have been listening to a lot of spiel for the last quarter of an hour, that I don't even know where I'm going, and that I'm there with arguments. Then I can get pissed off and let it fly out at the other person by saying: "What the hell are you telling me?" Really, the person who has got stuck is me. This is one of the things I try to avoid.

In short: I am flexible, I use doubt as an antidote to rigidity, and I love working with humor. I laugh all I can.

Joan Garriga: I agree with Ignacio on this matter of working with humor. For me, one of the important things when I work is enjoying myself, having a good time. I have observed that the only possible way for me to work is when I feel that I am enjoying myself, that it is a pleasure.

I think this can also be useful. For example, for type I it can be a model of flexibility, of fun, of capacity of enjoyment. This has happened to me with certain people in type I if I have managed to get into the relationship, to create the trust. . . because sometimes, if they are strong and active, or I feel that they are carping, or very orthodox, the relationship does not continue. I believe this would be one of the good things: flexibility, a sense of fun.

Another good point I think I have, as well as type VII in general, is being flexible with ideas, having a great capacity for moving ideas in all directions. So, the therapy can also have a persuasive side. It can invite the client to have new ideas and varied perspectives of things, to find better or more favorable points of view, something we in type VII do (perhaps as compensation) excessively well, often going beyond the limit between a more useful perspective and disingenuous self-deceit.

Another important aspect for me is connecting with my tenderness and my compassionate spirit, and seeing, in a form of quick regression, the child who is in pain and lost behind the patient's mask.

Also, when I dare, I see that it can be useful to get involved with my body. From that perspective I can be both maternal and protective as well as confrontational and firm. The dangers or difficulties I face are in the line of deceit, in giving the reins to my lack of faith, and from that perspective carrying the patient away on imaginary trips, or also by getting bored or losing interest, which sometimes leads me to withdraw internally from contact.

Laura Martinez: In principle, any preconceived idea bothers me, gets in my way. I think I feel really good when I am not expecting anything, or not looking for anything . . . when I'm simply there to see what's going on. That's when things happen! I don't know what . . . but something always happens.

Somehow I always try to place myself in a position of innocence, and for me innocence is "no-science." That is when I feel good. I don't like the word therapist either, or the concept of therapy, because it separates me a little, or a lot, from the other person. What I really feel is that we are each involved in a business that benefits us both, and that the healing process is mutual. The symptoms are things that are there to be seen, but in fact, they are a screen for the other things that lie behind.

Not that I have a great awareness of God or that I think of God in a clear, well-defined way, but sometimes I think there is a game that seems to be a divine game, since I started playing it, and that is the game of encounters.

Elena Revenga: My attitude as a therapist is similar to my way of participating in this discussion. Since I was told that I was going to be here I tried to prepare some ideas, make a few summaries, etc. When I got here, I forgot the few things I had prepared. I couldn't remember where I had them. So, usually I work without preparation. Neither do I keep clinical records. Sometimes my clients are surprised when I remind them, one year later, about an anecdote that is three years old. They never see me writing.

I think I take on a familiar attitude. I am cordial, sober, and embracing in the sense that everything they bring is fine—quite permissive and tolerant. That is a virtue and sometimes a trap that I set, because trust increases quickly. To begin with, I frustrate little, except when it is indispensable for trust. Sometimes, however, with frustration trust opens up. In general, I am usually quite permissive. Above all, motherly, with a touch of authority.

Paco Peñarrubia, Chairman: After this presentation we are going to deal with each one of the enneatypes. We will begin by talking of type I. First, the therapist representing type I, Antonio, will speak. After that, everyone else can participate, without any previous order, as things come up in the discussion.

THERAPEUTIC RELATIONS WITH TYPE I

Antonio Pacheco: My concern leads me to multiply my attention, i.e. my interest in the other person. When you, Elena, mentioned the matter of remembering something a client said last year about an event from three years back, I recalled scenes from six years ago. I don't write down notes either, although sometimes I draw up little outlines in order to follow the process.

I feel the matter of identification is very important. Today I find it gratifying and, I believe, quite productive to work with type I. But it didn't used to be like that. Before the Enneagram I felt an instinctive rejection. I saw my own rigidity reflected in the other person, and I didn't like it at all. Now, however, one aspect I have confirmed as efficient in helping type I is seeing and recognizing myself before him or her. I explain what I am like, which are my mechanisms, my crazy thoughts, my form of behavior, how I get around in life . . . .When the patient sees that I also have the same shortcomings he/she feels relieved, he/she opens up more easily, trusts, loosens defenses and gets more in touch with emotions, which is a great deal for type I.

Another aspect with regard to helping type I is giving them confidence, understanding, affection, sometimes in a paternal way. I think that for type I this is important in the sense of feeling understood, protected, supported, even respected as far as their rigid reasoning is concerned. Starting from there it is not too difficult to help them connect, on the basis of Gestalt or bodywork, and to help them begin to establish contact with all their deep childhood pain—with that child who has become so hard in order not to need; the child who is protecting him or herself with his/her rigidity and his/her points of reference; a child who has struggled to adapt, to be perfect, not to make any mistakes, in order to obtain affection and approval.

I think that the essential starting point would be to admit to the patient that, "I am just as crazy as you are," and be able to be open to unconditional acceptance. And from there, provide an adequate channel for the patient's own efforts to improve, to evolve.

Riccardo Zerbetto: Type II work with type I in a difficult relationship because there is a competition, a lack of trust. Although type II can seduce type I with their vitality, mobility, and greater flexibility, in the second phase of the therapy type I are critical about how type II deal with things and express themselves, perceiving an incongruous attitude and a false self. And there a complication, for the type I client, in this rivalry with the type II therapist. When the therapist does not feel the patient's (type I) total trust in him/her as a therapist, the latter may adopt a conflicting attitude, demanding this total trust.

Suzy Stroke: My experience with type I in general is very good. I like their punctuality, obedience, and organization, which are similar to mine. These qualities enable me to begin to work with them with greater ease.

I feel that I manage to conquer type I's trust starting from the intellectual sphere—somehow, showing them that, in general, I know more about them than they do themselves. Starting from that first intellectual moment I go over to making contact with the inner child, with emotions, with suffering.

When the patient has already begun to appreciate me as somebody who knows more than he or she does, the relationship is quite easy, and equal too. I feel that there is a mutual respect. I have never had any major problems with enneatype I.

Agueda Segado: I like this enneatype because they are organized, vital . . . because of their capacity for bringing to action tasks of an intellectual kind, etc.

I have had quite a lot of experience with type I, but always with women. The processes have, in some cases, been long, and in other cases the patients remained with me less than a year, on average. In these short processes it was the patients themselves who decided to leave the therapy, always when some difficulty with the work appeared, such as resistance to dealing with the paternal figure, etc. My experience is that these women have had a very bad relationship with their mothers and do not easily give up their power to another woman. It is even more difficult for them to feel a commitment and to surrender emotionally.

As I said, normally it is the patients themselves who decide, without any previous consultation or agreement, to leave the therapy. I have some examples of how they decide it is the best thing to do, and they do it in such a manner that, even though I may want to talk about it and be informed of the reason for their decision, it is not easy to know. They have simply made an irrevocable decision. In some cases they abandon the process when they have to question the paternal figure or, what amounts to the same thing, their system of values. In one specific case the patient reasoned: "I do not consider it necessary to revise my childhood." In another case the patient left the therapy because she was not achieving what she had come looking for: "A man." In all these cases I find it difficult to express to my patients that I feel hurt to see them abandon their process after having covered a good part of the way. Probably the expression of my emotion would help them get in touch with their emotional world.

In long processes the greatest difficulty I have come up against is integrating the person. They experience moments of very strong dissociation when they have to assume the responsibility for their feelings of hatred.

Annie Chevreaux: With regard to type I, I don't have much experience. I only have one patient belonging to this type. My first impression when I sat down in front of her—something which I still feel—was a great tension in my back. I got rigid. Her rigidity put me in touch with mine, and I tended to depreciate myself, as if she had caught me in a mistake. At the beginning of the therapy I felt inadequate, that she wasn't going to take me seriously. Sometimes I even doubted my professional capacity. When I realized this, I felt like provoking her: "You're behaving so nice and formal, so I'm going to do just the opposite." I would be rude on purpose, careless with my language, sprawling in my armchair. The realization that I was being rigidly delinquent in the face of her normative rigidity, like the two conflicting sides of the same matter, helped me create a more genuine contact with her. Now I feel that I have loosened up a lot, and when she acts like that, I laugh and touch her. Touching her helps her loosen up, while I relax when I feel that she is made of flesh and blood—not like that judge who paralyzed me and whom I provoked in order to avoid my fear of her.

Ignacio Lopez: I haven't found any male type I patients, either, only women. Perhaps the men would be a different matter, because I would connect in a different way, perhaps more along the lines of competition.

I remember a patient who came not long ago. She sat down on the chair and suddenly I felt my back was against the wall. She was like my father with a miniskirt. An incredible woman—good-looking, attractive and extremely well turned out, and blushing, as though she were about to burst at any moment. And there I was, feeling frightened.

To begin with, I never approach type I directly, however much they provoke my rebelliousness. (I already worked on that with my father.) I start off on an informal, tolerant level. With type I women, for example, I love being perverse and playful, bringing out all the playfulness of my perverse, sensual side. And I play around a lot in that respect.

I think that if they can trust me it is because I act the good boy's role. When they have a fit of anger I never go in head on. Instead, I make fun of them, for example, by saying: "Well, it looks like you can't stand a handful of wasps in your eye," or something like that. Reducing the drama, I can then go into the pain, to say: "That hurt you, that bothered you." I feel good with these women. As I say, I don't know what it would be like with the men.

I also have a great time with the business of saying dirty words. For example, when they come up with that puritanical language, and I say, "Oh! You're talking about a dick."

Joan Garriga: I have worked with quite a few people in type I. I remember a man with whom I only had one interview because I realized that he was too much for me. The first thing he did was name all the evils of the world, everything that had to be corrected in the world. Then he named all the evils of women and all that had to be corrected in women. Then he named all the evils of psychology and all that needed correction in psychology. Finally I asked him: "Well, you must have come here for some reason. What do you want?" And he answered: "Well, I'm here because my wife told me to come." He said it so implacably, as hard as iron . . . . He was like a jet-propelled rocket, talking about everything that was wrong, everything that needed correction; how something strong had to be organized in order to get rid of all the evils. I felt like a kind of tiny ant with nothing to do. I didn't even know what to lean on. I referred this person to a female type I therapist, and the fact is that they lasted three or four sessions. They got into a kind of fight and the type I therapist, who was weaker, was defeated.

What I feel with type I is that confrontation is of no use. When they come to me they make me feel small. I see myself saying: "Poor me, who am I next to this man—this very orthodox person who makes me feel weak?" Instead, I soften up, and perhaps, at certain moments, I show some weakness. They tolerate it, habitually, thus creating a link of trust, of complicity, and then I can bring out all my flexibility, all my humor, and also my rudest side. I break down this rigidity with a little madness, a little irony, with laughter.

I think that with type I the therapy begins to work, or is working, when they laugh openly. Then something is happening.

With type I women, I have observed their difficulty with depositing power in me. There is a very strong competition. The only way out that I have found is to become soft and gentle. If I get competitive something breaks.

Laura Martinez: I have had only one type I patient and he was a friend of mine. He asked me if he could attend a therapy group in order to learn how the thing worked. He soon began to connect with rage, and started to raze everybody to the ground. Nobody there dared to express a weakness or an emotion because he demolished, attacked, and cut people's heads off. In principle I like confrontation, so I began to fight him. But I think type VIII have their hands full with type I, because type I always reason with you, they never run out of patience. Somehow the strategy—what I discovered at the end (when I was exhausted)— was to express my emotion or my feelings to him. Then, the whole business was weakened for him.

Elena Revenga: When I have the feeling that the person belongs to type I, something has already happened to begin with. That is, I am usually quite undisciplined with time, so that I receive almost everybody late. So there they already know that they are going to have an imperfect therapist. When I realize that the patient is type I, I politely apologize for the delay and know that I am going to be subjected to an examination. This examination lasts for some time, and since I am already familiar with it, I usually pass. If I don't pass, the patient will leave for sure. If the patient stays, I have his or her trust.

When I am with type I (I have the virtue and the defect of entering completely into the other person and making the other person enter completely into me), I usually take into account what was the tremendous humiliation they suffered as children. I have the impression that type I's have been so mistreated, so humiliated as children, that I support them, I chat and talk. Besides, they are so clear in their reasoning, and there I am not going to get involved in any kind of fight. Instead, it is as if I slipped in underneath with a, "Well, you must have had such a rough time of it! You have had to build up so many lies! But what's the matter with you?" I usually go to the physiological level, that of physical sensation. Starting from there we go into the whole emotional side.

Paco Peñarrubia: (Answering a question from a person in the audience.) The feeling I am left with after listening to you is that what works best with type I is an understanding attitude, a little irony, questioning their values, and physical contact. The difficulty you have all referred to is this character type's rigidity.

Antonio Pacheco: I believe that the basic thing for working with type I, as a person belonging to type I, would be understanding, affection, and being very tolerant with their imperfections. That is, the support for their imperfections would also be a way of making them gradually let go of their rigidity . . . their obsession with doing things in such a conscientious way, and in order to win affection. The way to work with type I is by loving them, even if they make a mistake.

Paco Peñarrubia: What you say about loving understanding I think would hold for all the character types. More especially for type I than for the others? In short, then, it looks like in therapy with type I, what works well is to "de-educate" them as regards principles and educate them as regards sensitivity.

THERAPEUTIC RELATIONS WITH TYPE II

Paco Peñarrubia: I'm going to say something about type II. For me they are the most difficult patients, and my innermost feeling (I imagine that it is mistaken, but it's what I feel) is that these are people who do not get better because they do not come to get better.

My experience from working with many people in type II is that if I work from a behavioristic point of view (that is, helping them to change behaviors and aspects of their lives that do not work), they end up making use of those changes to manipulate the world better, not because they question themselves. Because of this resistance to questioning themselves I feel pretty tied down. This does not allow me to work deeply, on the level of an inner search, but rather on a more conventional level of improvement of symptoms.

I have had some patients who have experienced this difficulty or are going through it at the moment, whereas with the rest (most of them) I have found that they were not looking for an inner change, but a refinement of their seduction in order for things to work out better for them.

Riccardo Zerbetto: Type II deny that they have failed or gone wrong in the therapeutic relationship. Because of their mistrust, and that rivalry that makes them put themselves in a position of power, when they find the therapist who represents power from the point of view of his or her profession then a strong dependence on the therapist emerges, which the latter knows how to handle, and handles. In this handling, a relationship can appear that is longer and hypothetically more useful, although it can get stuck in a rut which has nothing positive about it.

73

The greatest pitfall I see is that the patient, with the old wound that needs to be replaced (like a need for love and recognition), does not easily accept a relationship in which he or she feels dependent. Hence, the patient tries to seduce you, creating a relationship in which he or she is also on the same level. And this seduction can be very powerful. There is an unconscious symbiotic function.

Type II have a deep wound that gets involved in the symbiotic, although conflicting, relationship. Thus, usually conflictive but strong relationships are created (and can last for a long time) in which the patient attempts to seize enough power to shift the relationship from a situation which is clearly one of balanced power (patient-therapist) to a relationship of love, or work, or a relationship of an intellectual nature, in order to balance the situation of power. I believe this is good if you know how to handle it, but it's difficult. As Ferenczi says, it is a matter of healing an old wound, and the patient needs to feel that he or she is loved, besides the fact that he or she is going to pay. The patient needs a totality without limits, although this is not explicit. It is an issue of compassion, then; a need for compassion before which the therapist can get stuck in not knowing how to reject and how much to dismiss as self-pity.

Antonio Pacheco: For me type II involve a very interesting relationship. I am married to a type II, and almost all my romantic experiences were with type II women. An intense, long love-hate relationship can be generated. They are usually the patients who last the longest.

Throughout the relationship there are periods of hatred and competitiveness, distance, seduction, approach, lies. I like their seductiveness. I have a good time. I also feel affectionate. But I always establish very clear limits that provide them with security.

One anecdote: In a group, a type II woman who was sitting next to me took hold of my hand and closed her eyes. She must have experienced a strong sensation on an emotional-sexual level. Afterwards, she said she felt ill. She denied she had felt anything. She felt guilty. She even vomited out of anguish. A few days later she worked on her sexual and emotional transference. The limits were clarified, and from then on the relationship improved noticeably. For her it was important to recognize her need and clarify the limits.

Suzy Stroke: I share your (Paco's) opinion about type II that not all, but mainly the women, come not for the therapy but because they have been sent there, or because the husband has been to therapy, and so . . . "Me too!" For reasons like that. But with the men, in general, it is quite a good relationship. I allow myself to be seduced; then I seduce, and from that moment things work out all right.

With the women it's very difficult and I feel that there must be something there that I do not manage to accept. Two things confuse me: their seductiveness, which probably makes me jealous (sometimes I would like to be able to seduce like that, and since I don't know how, I react a lot), and their lying. There is a continuous lying which I find difficult to understand. In principle I believe what they tell me, but when I realize that it was a lie it makes me very angry. For me they are the most difficult cases.

Agueda Segado: I have a great aptitude for pulling their lies apart and bringing them down to type IV, so they connect with their deficiency. Then they can see how they manipulate others instead of asking for what they need.

In my experience with type II women I have found that they had a great emotional deficiency with their mother, and a very idealized father.

My difficulty is that sometimes I believe their claims that they want to get better. But then a time comes when I begin to ask myself: "What isn't working in the process? Why aren't we making any headway?" I feel that I am failing. I have already swallowed their lies.

One example: With one patient I confronted all her lying, seeing that she wanted to be in therapy only to manipulate others better . . . in her own words: "To have more tools for dealing with others." When I pointed this out to her she said: "Don't touch me. I don't want to bring out my shit. I don't want to suffer. . . ." I carried on, confronting her with the fact that she didn't want to work, and she replied: "You have to work well with me because your prestige is at stake." At that point I could laugh because the issue was explicit.

I have observed that type II idealize their therapists a lot. They think that, by extension, the therapist is important. They also frequently show their aggressiveness and rivalry with women. In this case it is difficult for the patient to take on the responsibility for this rivalry and aggressiveness. I have the example of a patient who denied her rivalry with women, but always went out with men who had partners. Later on, she reached the conclusion that actually she did not like those men so much as the fact that they belonged to another woman.

Many people in type II come to therapy when their romantic affairs are not going well. But as soon as they find a partner or solve the matter, they abandon the therapy.

Annie Chevreaux: With type II I get on well. There is an affinity, and above all, a warm atmosphere is soon created. Their lies amuse me. I see them as something naive, childish. Under all that theatricality, I feel their fragility. I connect well with them. I like it when they like me. It's an honor for me!

The difficulty lies in confronting them because, if I feel that they like me, I am afraid of their not liking me. The craziest thing that comes to me now is that I am afraid that they will attack me if I confront them; that they will say that I am a brute; that I have no class, and so I will fall in disgrace. Probably, when I feel this way, they have managed to manipulate me, but I don't pay the slightest attention to this, because I believe that if I don't allow myself to be seduced there is no way of working with them. Besides, I can't find it in me to persecute them. I give them "six of one and half a dozen of the other," and above all, I use humor.

When, at the end of the session, they flatter me sometimes, stressing greatly how well-looked-after they have felt in anything that is the matter with them and in anything that seems so special to them, I usually reply that the thing they experience as something exceptional happens to a lot of people. "I'm sorry to tell you that you're not the only one!" Often they realize how theatrically they were behaving. When they burst out laughing, I know it has touched them—that they have realized, and we can carry on.

Another thing I want to point out is that I feel very free when working with them. I am always aware of the fact that the most probable thing is that they will leave the therapy when things get more involved. I work as if this were the last session we are going to have together. If I help them laugh at themselves, they cure me of my excessive internal demand.

Elena Revenga: I have little experience with type II men, more with women. Usually they try to seduce me with prestige: "I have chosen you. I have come to you. I hope to be the favorite." I don't usually pay any attention to this, and then they enter into rivalry, an aggression.

In the Enneagram this is the character type from which I receive the clearest negative transference. I also help them let it out. I let myself be seduced too . . . doing some seducing myself, on other occasions.

The process with type II is a "downward tendency"—like foreseeing depression. They go into depression, and come out of it, and go back in again. What I find exasperating is that after so much time they are still going around with "the great issue." They keep on bringing their great issue, that is, "their great problem." I say to them: "All right, now you know it. You know the way out. You've seen it. You've suffered. You've been in depression. But why don't you speak clearly for once!"

My mistake can be to become demanding and lose my patience. Entering into the demand of: "What more do you expect! I can't stay with you with your great issue any longer." This is where they get blocked. Getting out of there can take some time in order to recover the trust and, for me, to back out of my demands.

Laura Martinez: Since everyone has said such negative things about them, I want to say, in favor of type II, that I like them a lot. I find them very tender. Maybe the thing to do with them is to let them fail all they want. Perhaps because the ones I have had were drug addicts, and since that is a business in which you fail so many times . . . . But I love them.

Joan Garriga: I don't have much experience with type II, either. I have been working with a man for some time now, and we have reached a point in which he is systematically bringing out his enjoyment of the work with me, with a lot of flattering and all that. It produces an effect in me as if he were trying to create the atmosphere of a special relationship. I don't know whether it is to cover up his fear or his anger at not being the therapist. What I feel is that he tries to define the relationship as: "We are the two of us and that is great and that is all that's going on." My attitude towards this is to pay no attention. To keep silence, and see what will happen . . . which I don't know. He will either grow tired of it or he will get angry.

With the women . . . I wasn't aware of having had any type II female patients. Maybe I didn't realize it at the time. I suspect that I would get caught up in the seduction. I would get lost there. I would feel very tempted, especially if it were erotic seduction. I don't feel ready at this moment for dealing with that.

Ignacio Lopez: Nearly all the type II patients I have had were women, and I have also had some men. Both with the men and the women I feel that I work with seduction. I allow myself to be seduced by him or her. I really enjoy it, and I also act seductive, and very tolerant, to begin with.

I have had different types of experience. I can recall a type II who came as a dethroned princess. She was broken down after being abandoned, completely depressed for three or four years. The thing was to get out of that melancholy sadness, and it was hard work for me (this generally happens to me) to discover what was genuine emotion. I see three layers in type II. The first—a soft, seductive layer. I connect well. I seduce, we laugh, "Aren't you pretty!" They bring out all kinds of desires or fantasies in me.

There is a second, hard layer, which grates on me a lot—it is cold, calculating. With a type II in front of me I always have the feeling that they know well what is happening to me. It is as though I had to pierce through that in order to catch hold of that tender touch which I agree is fragile. It is as if I were dealing with a weak and frightened little child.

I think that from the basis of my fear I have a great ability for perceiving fear in type II. It is one of those character types with which I also work from the point of view of my fear. Type II can frighten me with that self-confidence, that way of lying so confidently. There is a point where I say: "Hell! That came out very confidently!" And then I say: "But, aren't you . . . ?" [in a way that contradicts or questions their lie or self-confident front.]

Another thing is "remote control" work with type II. This makes me feel uncertain, especially when it comes to confronting directly and saying: "I think that is . . . *whatever.*" That is a first-hand rejection. The patient goes home to come back the next week saying: "Oh, look, that is like that . . . and so forth." Sometimes I handle this badly.

Now I feel good working with type II. I went through a period in which it was difficult for me because they made me feel rebellious. Now, the cases I am in charge of have been going better for some time.

Paco Peñarrubia: My conclusion here is less clear than the previous one. It looks like working with type II is especially comfortable for types V and VIII, above all. Anything to do with their having a greater ability for spotting lies?

It seems that, independently of that capacity for empathy that can be present, what works best, from what I have heard you say, is to connect with the most fragile part, with deficiency. From there the barrier of competitiveness and haughtiness can be overcome.

THERAPEUTIC RELATIONS WITH TYPE III

Suzy Stroke: For me it is quite easy to work with type III. I greatly enjoy it because I feel a strong desire to give to this person what I would have liked to have received, but did not, and had to discover on my own.

Because of their capacity for adapting and their ease in any situation, when they come to therapy, type III try to see what it's like, "What's going on here? What do I have to do?" When you begin to work and confront the more obvious things, type III immediately go ahead of the therapist and lay out all the games that they did not imagine to be so clearly visible to begin with. But since they are visible, their next strategy is—"I'll tell you everything before you get to it." In this way they easily distract the therapist. "I'm already top of the class, grade A; everything is honky-dory." And the therapy continues without anything real happening. They are so good at adjusting to the therapist's wishes that it seems that everything is fine. (All my personal therapies were like this. They came to an end at this point.)

In working with type III, I let that part go by. Then I give the patient precisely what he or she wants the most, but also fears the most—the encounter with someone who really sees him or her, somebody who knows what there is to be found (because the client probably does not trust even him or herself). I do this with great care, and using my own story, using all the places I have been to. Then it is possible to create a good vehicle for work. This is where I feel that the characteristic traits of type III— of responsibility and really wanting to get somewhere—come out and are put to good use. The patients benefit enormously. So these are the situations I handle best, and where the results are very good.

As Claudio was saying, I feel that in other kinds of human relations, also, I have a good relationship with type III, especially with the women. There is a connection, an interaction, and an identification in which a lot of things take place—not so much with the men, but with the women. After having lived a great part of my life in competition with women in general, today I feel I have achieved genuine friendships. As Lola Ansola said to me today: "One of the things in my life in which I did not have to make great efforts has been our friendship." It works, and is highly gratifying and precious to me.

Agueda Segado: In my experience with type III, the most difficult thing for me is overcoming, at the beginning of the therapy, the competitive wrestling matches they subject you to. Each one does it in a different way, but they all do it.

One example: I had a patient who in the second session, as a threat, said to me: "I am a black belt." If you show them that you don't care, even that you aren't afraid, or that, there is something more important than competing, they get involved, they trust you, although this happens little by little, and slowly. I am not scared of type III's trying their strength on me, although sometimes it hurts. I see the frightened child they carry inside themselves.

My greatest difficultly with type III is related to their degree of narcissism, but I suppose that happens in any character type, and not only in III.

I have had greater difficulties when working with men, and that is because I forgive them less easily than the women for their vanity, their frivolity, their being so preoccupied with their image. In one case, I even empathized more with the patient's internal object—his partner—than with the patient himself, so that I provoked in him a negative transference towards me.

The common factor in my work with type III is that I have always found their inner world to be desolate, and in certain moments I have felt genuine fear for the person: that he should be able to go through so much pain without losing his mind. For me that is the most difficult point of the therapeutic process. The person feels genuine fear and mistrust that you are going to make him do the same thing his parental figures did—cross the desert, feel emptiness and loneliness. These are the difficult moments of the process. Beyond these difficulties, the relationship is usually warm.

Annie Chevreaux: With type III, in the beginning, the relationship isn't easy. I feel there is a lot of coolness and it is hard to break the ice.

The difficulty I run into with them depends on the subtype. With sexual type III I get on well. We feel warmly towards each other. With social and self-preservation type III, things are more complicated for me, as if there were a wall between them and me.

Sometimes, without realizing it, I put myself on a level of demand—of being efficient with them. I have to be careful to see if they are really involved, or if they are merely doing the "gym exercises" I am telling them to do in order to grow as soon as possible, or in order for me to tell them that they are doing wonderfully well, rather than to discover something that is useful for themselves.

Ignacio Lopez: Type III is a character type which I find very comfortable to work with. (In general, I am comfortable with types II, III, IV.)

I do experience one initial difficulty. Earlier on I was telling my colleagues that I have the feeling that I acquire a lot of information with my eyes, and that I give a lot of information about myself, both of my affection and my rejection, with my eyes. But, type III's eyes are eyes in which I see nothing. They are eyes into which I look, to begin with, and it is as if my gaze bounces back from these eyes. They return me, or I have that feeling of emptiness, which I later recognize as the feeling of emptiness which type III's have hidden inside themselves. Starting from there I can make a connection, as well as with seduction, almost always.

For example, in the case of a man I know who is quite young, I am like his permissive Daddy. But, I make it clear to him what I like and what I don't like, and I keep him on a string. In the case of the women, I work a lot with humor. I find it funny when they get into that "gym business," trying to be good. Not long ago, with a female patient, I said to myself: "I don't know if I am doing this really well, because this woman's capacity for realizing is amazing." She caught onto everything, one thing after another. A high level of efficiency! That is where I can get stuck, in the sense of "I'm doing great"—like enhancing myself. If I get down from there, I can begin to appreciate whatever comes out, however little it may be. I can see the little girl hiding behind, or the little boy.

Joan Garriga: What happens to me with type III, especially with the women at the beginning, is that when I look at them it is as if I could not see their soul. I feel them as objects. Then this really sadistic thing comes out—of wanting to rape, break, tear, destroy. It is an initial impulse. After that I try to look and see what the little girl inside is like. What I see is a great desolation, or a little girl who was never looked at, who was never seen. Sometimes, in the face of this, I start to really look. To look inside her. To have a more genuine contact, up to where this is possible.

With time, I have felt that the greatest difficulty for type III is admitting openly, and without beating around the bush, that they are people in need. It has proved important for them to feel that I *need*, if not *them*, then other people; that I have needs. It is important for them to feel, little by little, that they can express their needs, that they can need something. I am being tender and careful with them.

What I see as most important with type III is that they should never, ever, be humiliated. They are afraid that, "If I become a little weaker, you're going to humiliate me, you're going to be superior to me." For me the key is to stand on an equal basis and remain in my own authenticity, truthfully.

Laura Martinez: Something quite similar has happened to me. What I use in these cases is: "If you confess now, I'll confess afterwards." For type III it is a little like being in the confessional, especially when they have a story they have difficulty in bringing out.

They amuse me. I feel they are very playful. It is like playing in a mirror-maze with them, and with a little humor, the thing works.

Elena Revenga: With type III, I have two possibilities. It is important to keep my eyes open from the start. I don't like to say this, but for me it's like looking at the person's quality and getting the feel of how far you can go. I have frequently run into type III's with clear symptoms, whose interest and commitment was to cure the symptoms in order to then leave. That is the maximum demand, and that's that. If I have a clear idea of this, in a short period of time I feel efficient. It is easy to solve the matter. Yet, I am left with a feeling of dishonesty. That is where I can't be at ease unless I open the doors and say: "Well, we've solved this, but this, this and that still remains." That is one possibility.

The other possibility is that I work better with type III if, instead of the tête-à-tête situation of individual therapy, they are in a group. If we have such an intimate relationship, just the two of us together, my tendency to support, to embrace, to be maternal, would betray me. Keeping them there staring into their emptiness for ages and ages is hard for me.

My experience, especially with type III women, is that they make their way on their own in group therapy, almost without my interfering, or without interfering directly. I suppose that is the easiest way for me to work with emptiness. Otherwise, I tend to get involved in too much intimacy.

Antonio Pacheco: I want to add two things. With type III, I let myself be, and then a relationship of a certain complicity is born, a relationship of being on their side in order to slowly get behind the mask. But, this comes to a point, a limit, and I run out of it. Then I feel they are cold, and besides, it seems like they understand everything at once and do not want to go into things any deeper. In the face of my limitations in individual work, I resort to inviting them to take part in a group. If they accept, the work improves. It seems like they can take the group work as a personal challenge, and confrontation becomes easier. In any case, I don't have so much experience with type III.

Riccardo Zerbetto: With type III, things look pretty easy to begin with, although there is also a game of double seduction which can facilitate an easy preliminary phase, and afterwards a more superficial one in which there is a competitive game of "Who is more seductive?" Here the therapeutic process can get held up. If the type II therapist has done sufficient work on himself or herself, it can be a good aid to getting out of that relationship of superficial contact and getting in touch with his or her own thing, and also being a good model for the patient.

Paco Peñarrubia: I will say that my difficulty with type III coincides with what you have said about lack of authenticity—the mechanical side—and how to create trust.

My temptation is to leave them alone because I feel that they are leaving me alone. I'll explain. The person I have in front of me isn't there. My risk is saying: "Well, I'm not here either. I don't believe you." The antidote is precisely to break through this abandonment, this lack of real presence, and begin to accompany that emptiness.

Sometimes I have to imagine the real person behind the mask—that one whom the other person doesn't even know or suspect—in order to be able to get near their emptiness. That is the most difficult part in working with type III: guiding them towards the terrifying void of looking at themselves in a mirror and not seeing anything, not even their own face, but instead, a landscape without limits or shapes, sometimes a charred, black landscape. It isn't easy to get there, and I have needed a lot of commitment, warmth and frustration in order to learn to accompany them.

THERAPEUTIC RELATIONS WITH TYPE IV

Agueda Segado: I find it easier to work with the tenacity type IV, and less with the shame subtype, since it is hard for me to stand the whining. I can't always empathize with the patient.

I have observed that type IV find it easier to deal with the maternal figure and more difficult to deal with their paternal figure, since it has been idealized.

I think I have a great ability for bringing out their delirious ideas—the crazy notion that they are unique. If I let the idea flourish, the person gathers great strength from it, and later on I lead them to accept that they are the same as others, not different from them.

As for their voracious side, their envy, their feelings of destructiveness, etc., I am permissive. I listen to them with naturalness, making them feel that it is normal for them to have those feelings, even towards me. "Nothing's the matter, it's normal. . . ." Like it is something we all have, and nothing is the matter. In short, I put it over to them that they have the right to have those feelings. What I do take great care of is that they see that they are not only that ugly part, but that they also have other positive aspects, such as loving feelings, etc. I help them integrate "the ugly part" when there is some solid or good side to lean on.

The most difficult thing for me is not to get caught up when they start attacking me with the money, or in other ways. They do this with the purpose, among other things, of being punished, as a way of feeling that I am paying attention to them.

The advantage of working with type IV is that I understand them very well. The greatest difficulty is that I have little patience for the complaining type IV. I feel that I work better with those who have the same instinct as me.

Suzy Stroke: I do fine with type IV to begin with. The therapy I conduct always has a beginning and an end, and the end is already determined when the therapy begins. During the first part, we work and everything flows. When we start reaching the end, the problem arises with the pattern, "I don't want to finish." That is the difficulty.

Somehow, due to my own tendency of having to finish what I begin (not only because I work in this type of therapy, but also because I, as a person, see life as something which does not always have to be lived in manipulative and self-imposed suffering, for this is not what it's all about), I manage to change that system of beliefs a little, and make type IV begin to see that life does not always have to involve suffering and dependence on others. These are elements that bog them down and make them persist with the game of not wanting to finish the therapy.

Antonio Pacheco: Type IV is one of the character types I identify with best in therapy. I believe it has to do with the connection between types IV and I in the Enneagram. Often in my life I have felt like type IV, in envy, in suffering, in comparison, in dependence, in victimism.

Furthermore, I think that my side of order, structure, control and perfectionism can help them as a healthy way out.

I remember an anecdote from work: In one group there was a type IV patient who, whenever she was going to speak, would start out by crying, systematically. I didn't know what to do to stop her from amplifying her emotion. One day I came up with the idea of placing a box of tissues before her before she started speaking. She held back her tears and got angry with me. She promised not to cry anymore. It seems that from then on she began to take on more responsibility for her emotions, realizing her dramatization, suffering, and victimism.

For some people in type IV it has been interesting to keep an emotional or dream diary, and to meditate systematically.

Riccardo Zerbetto: With type IV there is normally an easy connection to begin with. For type IV, all that is valuable lies outside themselves, and type II (my type) is "Everything in me." They complement each other quite automatically, and easily involve the process of idealizing the therapist, which can be good in an initial phase, in which idealization is frequent. The matter gets more complicated if the type II therapist hasn't worked on his or her own character type. If the relationship stays on this level of idealization, it will without any doubt turn into destructiveness. Type IV can't remain satisfied with the business of valuable things being outside themselves, so the therapist has to be an expert in progressive frustration, and in gradually rejecting this power that type IV, with their projection, leave to him or her. Thus, the work involves frustrating this projection, and supporting self-reliance, self-esteem.

Ignacio Lopez: Type IV is the character type that brings out my sadistic streak to the highest degree. Almost all my experience has been with women. Right now I can't remember any men. I have noticed differences with the subtypes. With sexual type IV, I need little to get into a fight. I am not happy about how things have gone. They hang me up a lot, not from the point of view of seduction, but from that rivalry, that competitiveness, from that: "I bet you anything that you won't cure me." The bad thing is that I get involved in this, and they are right.

On the other hand, with the other two subtypes I feel better. They also bring out my sadistic streak, but it is much gentler, and I can handle it. I treat them ironically. I laugh or suddenly repeat their model: "Please look at me a little, you haven't looked at me once in the whole session." I can allow myself a lot and I feel that they tolerate it well. That makes things easier.

Joan Garriga: I also really enjoy therapy with type IV, and find that it is quite fun. I have learned a lot from type IV, especially with regard to being so hungry and feeling the pain and the emptiness in such a heartrending, piercing way. (Something I could not imagine.) I have learned this from them, and it moves me a lot, and brings me nearer to them.

What I do with type IV is that in the first sessions I nip certain manipulations in the bud, so that they do not repeat themselves in the future. I remember one case who said to me, in the first session, "Well, I have tried to commit suicide a couple of times and I don't know if I'm going to try it again." I said: "There are two things here. Those who commit suicide don't come back, and those who try to commit suicide can't come back because I don't want them to" –in the sense that, "You don't have any intention of working if you try to commit suicide." This has worked well.

It has also worked out well because I have become curious about type IV. I understand the cognitive structure of the matter more and more. I can give it back to them so they understand what they are doing, i.e. what their resignation is like, what their anger is like, their provocation, their difficulty in accepting love, and all their maneuvering, which I do not like very much.

Laura Martinez: Type IV's, in general, are too much for me. They are real cry-babies, and especially if there is a victim. (There is somebody who is receiving that continuous pain.) What happens to me is that I get angry. I start yelling and I throw them out. Once this worked really well. I shouted my head off and the patient did not come for two weeks. When he returned I apologized because I had gone a bit too far. He told me that it had done him a lot of good. He had a partner who had AIDS, and he (the patient) was always crying. That continuous crying did not allow the kid to develop his story or stay calm.

In general, things end up really badly with type IV.

Elena Revenga: With type IV there is a special relationship, perhaps it is a type that is my opposite. That is what makes things work. I am very undramatic, and type IV are far more dramatic. Neither do I usually get involved in competitiveness, and they are brought face to face with their own selves without having to do almost anything.

I am usually patient when they come with their complaints. Then I limit their time, and as the sessions go by I let them complain a little less. Sometimes I set a limit for their complaints in each session.

Something I don't say, but which is present (with type IV) is something like: "Nothing that you have experienced as so terrible is going to destroy me." That is where trust emerges. "Those things that for you are so destructive and terrible do not destroy me," but not because I am omnipotent. Simply "No." From here there is a process of cognitive replacement. I think that this is the best way for type IV to be integrated.

Paco Peñarrubia: Where it seemed to me that the greatest difficulty was to be found is (as Laura said) when the relationship concentrates on the sadistic aspect, between type VIII and type IV's masochism. It would be better to work from rapport, on the basis of a greater understanding, and also with the cognitive aspect, so they understand themselves better and "feel" themselves less.

What works well for me with type IV is to put over to them the attitude of not punishing their orality, while putting myself in my place, so that they do not devour me or feel guilty for trying it. Something like: "It's not bad to be hungry. The only thing is that I don't let myself be eaten up . . . and that is what we are going to work with."

The entire suffering part I prefer to turn into terms of orality: "Instead of saying you are having a rough time, look at it as if it were a fit of hunger." I feel that this is the way to begin to build from inside.

THERAPEUTIC RELATIONS WITH TYPE V

Annie Chevreaux: Sitting before type V patients I feel a strong urge to shake them, to make them understand that they are not immortal, that they have to get going. Type V's bring out my type VIII, moving them and all that.

Sometimes I am afraid of going too fast with them and I say to myself: "What if I don't have the same patience people had with me when I started my own therapy?" I know, because of what happened to me, that it is more a question of uncovering the rage. With pain, to begin with, there is nothing to be done. I try to get them pissed off as soon as possible. I think it is the most curative thing for type V.

Antonio Pacheco: With type V, I have had little experience. Normally, in the session, a barrier comes between us which I do not know well how to overcome. Especially when they get rational, with their idealizations, with their mysteries, their deliriums, I don't know how to help them connect, open up, get out of their coldness. In the face of my difficulty with the individual work, I invite them to work in a group. There the relationship changes considerably. All you have to do is respect their rhythm and little by little they open up and reveal themselves.

Riccardo Zerbetto: With type V, I have big fights because it is like conquering a castle. The more closed up type V are, the more defensive they are, the more difficult it is for the type II therapist to stay calm with not seducing the princess in the castle. It is a good character type to work with as long as the conquest is not the end of the process, but as a moment— something to facilitate this empirical investment, this useful investment, also financial.

Since type V are quite difficult and type II are very seductive, this can be a useful tool. The difficult matter here is also the final phase, further ahead in the process, in which type II is frequently going to be disappointing as regards his or her seductive promise. It is possible that the client is disappointed, and shuts himself or herself in even more, especially in view of the omnipotent attitude of the type II therapist, who likes conquering but is not sufficiently fond of the more subtle task of introjection.

Suzy Stroke: I love them. I sense the fascination of the mystery behind that totally listless, extinguished appearance. This seems to come out of me spontaneously. If type V feel that someone is fascinated by them, they open up. They are never clear; they are always as if in hiding, with very little self-esteem; and suddenly they come for help. When they feel that somebody is drinking from their source, it works well. A link of trust is created, which is the most difficult thing with type V. With trust as a basis it is easy. Yet I have to be extremely careful. Apart from the individual sessions, there is also the group therapy, and there you can't have any kind of confrontation—nothing that can hurt type V.

They have a tremendous hyper-sensitivity. With affection and firmness they can surrender themselves to the therapy. I really like them. I am patient and I always take care that nothing happens that might close them again and rebuild resistances.

Agueda Segado: After revising my work with type V, I have realized that, without setting out to do so, what I have worked on most with them is their relationship with the working world and with men (especially with type V women). In the case of a sexual type V patient, I worked on not only his commitment with work, but also his feeling of hatred as strength.

I have no difficulties in leading them to connect with emptiness—despite their fear of disintegration—and from there, to the flow of the emotional world.

What I think has produced the best results with type V is keeping up a loving and unconditional attitude, in such a way that when they withdraw or disconnect and then come back, I am there with them without criticism or censorship. This, together with the explicit demonstration of my love for them, helped them, in certain cases, to enter into that highly painful world of their relationship with their mother.

My difficulty lies in the moments in which they get up on the pedestal. I can feel inadequate and somewhat afraid of how to treat them.

Ignacio Lopez: I have little working experience with type V. For me, type V is the character type that I find most difficult to love, and this creates more difficulties. They put me in a tight spot and I have to be on guard all the time. It is tiring work. They bore me, they distract me. I don't feel good. When the session is over I say to myself: "Well, what the hell has this guy done? I was fine when I started and now I feel awful." In the next session I give it right back to him.

Insofar as I am involved in that war, I do start loving my type V patient. To the extent to which he or she is able to put things outside himself or herself, against me, I can find affection.

Joan Garriga: I also have little working experience with type V. What happens to me is that I get impatient. What I feel is that type V find it hard to let things out, and I get lost. I lose my patience and it doesn't work.

Also, what I feel in the group, sometimes, is that I start saying nonsense and somewhat risky things. I get the impression that they are frightened and close up even more. I feel that I just can't deal with them.

Laura Martinez: With me, it depends. There are type V's who are easy to love directly and to give affection to, easy to have talk to you. But there are other V's who are in their heads all the time. Not long ago a type V patient said to me: "I don't love my mother but I'm going to spend three days with her in a health spa. I want to patch things up with her so that she doesn't die without my having sorted the matter out." We worked for a while and finally she said to me: "Oh! So then it's a matter of *giving*." And I said to her: "Very good." And she replied: "And then what?"

Elena Revenga: After despairing with type V, I realized that the worst thing I could do with them was to demand things of them. Whenever I can, I stick to something like: "Every time you look for my eyes they will be there for you, and with those eyes I recognize your existence." Like a recognition of existence for itself. "I don't demand anything of you."

I call therapy with type V, "the therapy of find me out." They are continuously putting themselves in the situation of, "You, as a therapist, have to find me out." I also find that they are continuously putting me to the test. It is like: "I'm still not sure if that recognition of yours of my existence, which could be similar to love, is genuine." It is a process of great patience, until, when you least expect it, they come and open up. Probably it is something they have been feeling for some time, but they do not show it until they are completely sure.

I did experience a lot of blocking when, before that emptiness, I made demands on them. But it works much better for me the other way: "I am not going to find you out completely, but every time you look for my eyes they will be there for you." It is support, and an unconditional presence, but with great respect for their space, with a little distance.

Antonio Pacheco: I am going to read something written by a type V in which he tells it to me in a few words, but clearly.

"I saw you as somebody much more distant, colder, and more of a judge. As if you didn't express anything of yours, especially in the individual sessions. Little by little this has changed." (He changed over to the group. I couldn't handle it, there was a barrier.) "My feeling was that I had to reveal myself in order for you to reveal yourself, and so I didn't trust you. Little by little you have gradually revealed yourself, and I have gradually got to know and accept you. Now I see you much nearer, but at the same time I see or feel your limitations with me, and I say: 'This is not the right therapist for me.' It is as though you will never be able to understand me altogether. It is like, first you have to surrender yourself to me and then do what I want you to do. Well, I surrender myself little by little. Before there was much more hatred, but everything has gradually changed, and now, above all, there is love, and quite a lot of sincerity. I have felt understanding, tenderness, the desire to hug you, throughout this change. Each time I feel more interested, and it is much easier for me to open up to others and to you. I think I will remain for the rest of my life in this conscious growth."

And I have done nothing. I only had a lot of patience.

Paco Peñarrubia: It looks like the greatest difficulty arises when the therapist faces the coldness, and there is no way to get around it. Things work better when this can be done.

These are patients that I like a lot. I find their sensitivity gratifying. Their capacity for realizing things, their anti-authoritarianism—I like all this about them. The feeling I have is that I am a good blind man's guide for them in the world; I am a good supplier of faith in the world. In exchange, I have learned a lot from them in the inward journey. So, I feel indebted to them. There is a giving and receiving I often experience with type V that does not happen to me with the other character types, and that explains the gratification.

THERAPEUTIC RELATIONS WITH TYPE VI

Ignacio Lopez: My work with type VI is ambivalent, as is logical. There are people in type VI who bore me enormously and others with whom I have a good time. In general, with type VI I enjoy myself more and more. I think I work with them as a mirror, and with a lot of humor. There is irony on both sides. From there, everything can be moved—the fear, the penalization.

I always start working with type VI from a soft, vulnerable perspective. That is when I think they get caught up. Then it is a question of denouncing whatever appears, such as fear, doubt; or when desire appears I clarify it: "Because what you would like is . . . *whatever.*"

I think I have more difficulty with the duty type VI. I see them as the most rigid of the three subtypes. I find it hard work to break down that wall. I find them quite tough. They are the ones I deal with the worst.

Joan Garriga: I also enjoy working with type VI. Their anguish, their suffering, move me quite a lot. I try to bring bodywork in a bit, for things to be a little warmer, so they find themselves in their simplest and most physical aspects. Type VI have greatly developed the observer's dissociation as a means of controlling fear.

The task is making the weak type VI feel less guilty, and providing some rest to the counter-phobic type VI so that they sense me as a strong person and can rest there a little, elaborating their fears and associated difficulties.

Laura Martinez: With types VI and VII, I have a kind of vacuum. I don't have any type VI patients. I had one not long ago whom I treated as a type VI, but I think she was type VII. It went fine as long as we worked on doubt with courage and all that. When I started seeing that the wind blew in a different direction, that in fact what was the matter was that she wanted everything, and that the questions of doubt really meant that she didn't want to give anything up . . . when I began to suggest the question of sobriety, she disappeared.

Elena Revenga: I think I find it restful to work with type VI. I think I seduce the warm type VI. With the duty type VI, I swim with the current, and then with irony I try to change the rigid accent. With the strong ones I act as if they were seducing me. For a certain period of time I listen attentively, I understand, etc. Little by little, brain-racking is substituted with self-observation. What often happens is that I work as if they were children—with bodywork. And, starting from the bodywork, I move into the emotional aspect.

Annie Chevreaux: I understand type VI well. I feel intellectually close to them. I understand what is the matter with them, and now I am discovering something new. Now that I am far more aware of fear at the emotional level, I can accompany them better. This is what makes my work with them easier. Nevertheless, what I find hard to deal with is type VI's invulnerability, the strong type VI, and especially the women.

I had a strong type VI woman as a client and things worked out badly. Now we're going to take it up again. I made a mistake in something I asked her to do—a job outside the session. I made a mistake. I apologized to her and she has taken advantage of this to seize my power as a therapist. She would call me at home as if I were her friend. I felt more and more attacked. She didn't bat an eyelid. She didn't turn a hair. And, she was unable to listen to me when I told her the extent to which I felt attacked by her. I felt that I was losing my grip more and more, that soon I was going to tell her to go to hell, that I was going to hang up on her. I was left with the feeling that I had been the attacker and the one who was out of control.

Now she is coming back. Maybe it wasn't so bad that I lost control, which was my great fear. I have faith that something may have happened, that perhaps I have helped her see that you can lose control. But anyway, we'll see . . . .

Agueda Segado: I have observed that, in a session, many people belonging to type VI don't begin to work until they have tried to cut my head off. How do they do this? By, "I'm not getting better." "This is no good." "I feel helpless," etc. If I don't get involved in any of these games, they can begin to work. Sometimes, when a patient remains for a long time in this helplessness and passive rebellion, I'm the one who ends up being helpless.

I like the strong type VI. Until now what has worked best with them has been my loving and unconditional attitude, and not being afraid of them. In this way, when they attack me, want to burn down my office, etc., I am permissive with their destructiveness, with their fireworks, even when they cut my head off. When this happens, I am all there, alive, and the person is grateful to me for it. I could sum it up as: "This is not what matters most."

I am not afraid of their confrontational side, but I find it hard going when they stay in passive rebellion—in the powerlessness of nothing being right, of there being no solution for them. Sometimes they exasperate me, although I also know that the best thing is to hand them back a literal rendering of what they are expressing, or give them back emptiness.

I have little patience for the seductiveness of the warm type VI, or for their massive dependence. I have the case of a patient who, when I put some distance between us and stopped looking at him continuously, began to lose energy, as if everything he had achieved in therapy had been made possible because he had my eyes on him. I was frightened by such a massive dependence, until I was able to understand that he needed those speculative eyes on him.

In general, I have a gift for bringing out the bad, aggressive little boy they have inside, and for removing the punishment for aggression so that they can experience the latter as strength.

Suzy Stroke: Since my way of thinking is very simple, I often manage to keep type VI company in their endless elaborations, and somehow, despite them, I simplify their lives. The warm and duty subtypes generally awaken my maternal side, but with the strong subtype, the sexual ones, I have to be careful, because that is where positive counter-transference arises. Sometimes I do not see it or perceive it until much later. It has been the only type that has attracted me in the therapeutic relation, and where I have not caught myself being seduced, without my realizing, until some time later. Knowing this, I have to be careful. Nevertheless, I can make them trust me and bring out their fear and pain, mainly because of the strong and clear confrontations, together with pointing towards the possible way out.

Antonio Pacheco: The warm type VI bring out my fatherly instinct—the desire to protect them, support them, cheer them up, remove their guilt. I think this is good help to begin with. It also helps them to begin to see and recognize themselves.

With the strong type VI there is usually a competitive relationship, which I find uncomfortable, especially when it appears in a group. If I can remain in a stronger position, the relationship can work, but otherwise it is shaky. This has already happened to me a couple of times. The patient felt superior and then left.

When I have kept the role of authority, the patients can end up adopting a submissive position, or more than submissive, an accepting role—opening up, without competing, without fighting. Although, in my experience, it seems difficult to make them connect with their emotions. Bodywork is good for them.

Riccardo Zerbetto: With type VI there is also a relatively easy connection for me because type II acts vitally, with courage, breaking the rules, breaking the limits. This is a model that can attract type VI's energies. This attraction also depends on whether the type II therapist has dealt with his/her own type— that is, his/her compulsion to conquer the other.

Paco Peñarrubia: Type VI looks like the easiest type to work with, except in Laura's case, which can be perfectly understandable, since type VIII is a more frightening character for type VI. On the other hand, I imagine it must also be fascinating. With type VI it looks like there is an aptitude for working, and in different ways. However, you have spoken more of the process when it works well, and I haven't heard you mention what happens when they cut the therapist's head off. How do you react?

In my case, I usually give them security in the initial phase, and then afterwards I confront them more. Their paralysis frustrates me considerably, and sometimes I react with patience, at other times I push them into action. I usually forbid the word "confusion" because it seems to me to be a smoke screen with which they amuse themselves and distract me. When the patient says: "I'm confused," I ask him or her to use another, more emotional word. "I'm sad, or angry," or whatever.

In the "head-cutting" phase I usually eliminate their guilt, letting them experience that nothing is going to happen if they express their negativeness. In fact, I have run physical risks (fights, etc.) so they could learn to *experience* conflict instead of fantasizing about it.

THERAPEUTIC RELATIONS WITH TYPE VII

Joan Garriga: It seems to me that my relationship with type VII patients has evolved a great deal according to my relationship with myself. Some years ago, I believed that type VII and health were pretty similar things.

I admit that type VII used to seduce me. Now I don't believe them. I don't believe anything. I sift everything. I experience something similar to what you were saying before, Suzy, about type III. I get this compassionate thing for them. I understand them. They also bore me. There is a point where I feel boredom. What I try to do with type VII is make things very clear, providing clear frameworks.

I don't confront type VII. I find this hard to do. I think this is a kind of identification with the other person. I am afraid of wounding them, as if I could see a lot of pain inside myself from receiving the wound. So, I am gentle but quite forceful when providing the framework. I don't let them get away with a lot, but make things stay in their places.

Sometimes I also let them talk, and then I say: "All right, very good, now be quiet. What do you feel? What is the matter with you? Breathe. . . . " Whatever. In a gentle way I try to differentiate the spiel from reality. That is: "This is your story, now let's look for the real thing," so they can start creating the idea that their story is in one place, but in another place they can find a more genuine, more real experience.

I also think that the important thing for working with type VII (and where I feel that I have improved considerably) lies in the capacity for receiving their pain. I believe this is the key. If the therapist is available for them to fall into pain, to fall into the feeling of what they haven't had, of what they have missed, and is able to accompany this, the therapy works.

Elena Revenga: This is the type that I find most complicated. Since they seduce on all sides, I always have to keep establishing limits. The problem is that, if the limits are excessively harsh, the thing doesn't work. I have to discover which is the point at which I feel comfortable (not too invaded), and the point at which the other person is friendly enough to be able to allow himself or herself to experience pain. It is difficult to get to this encounter. I am afraid that I am going to be endowed with such a degree of friendship that I am burdened with this prejudice. I am cautious with this tug-of-war regarding limits.

My experience with some people in type VII tells me that when we delve into the pain I am greatly moved. It is like a desert in pain, similar to type V, similar to what type V keeps quiet. But, type VII have such a capacity for reorganizing afterwards, and for running away as soon as they can, that I get hung up in an intimate secret with them when we have gone down there. I feel betrayed, because as soon as they can, they get away. I don't know many people in type VII who have been constant in a long, individual process. I, at least, am left feeling like a part of history, left with that common experience we have both been in. But, I feel a little worried about what is going to happen.

I like to see them after some time. If they have suffered a depression, I say to myself: "That's a good sign!"

Ignacio Lopez: My experience with type VII is similar to Elena's. In my case, at least at the moment, I think type VII is the character type that presents me with the greatest problems, but not so much as regards discovering the emotional side. Rather, it is like getting on a level of hyper-attention—the kind of therapy where I say: "Hell, this one should pay twice as much!" because they keep me on my toes. Like traps, tricks, suddenly they take me to Neptune with an argument. They go down, then they go up once again. I find it really hard work. I can get pissed off. They seduce me, or I seduce them, but then it turns out that the purpose of this seduction is to become my friend! I don't know, it's amazing. It requires a great, great deal of attention. I find it tiring. It can piss me off, and from my anger I confront them. When I confront them, the thing begins to work better, but it still is tiring. They leave, they disappear, they come late. It is all very complicated, very much on a level of alert. I have enough of that already!

Annie Chevreaux: I have a great affinity with my type VII patients. What I see is their sensitivity, their fragility. I know that they can break. I feel the need to treat them well. The thing is that sometimes there is a lot of familiarity. There is a narcissism that is common to types V and VII, due to interests, to sensitivity. In fact, a kind of pact of respect is created, a pact of non-aggression, making it more difficult for me to confront them more.

I remember the case of a patient who felt guilty with regard to his mother, a controlling mother . . . and with his girlfriend. He had both of them against him. I helped him a great deal to undo this, to become a man, to be a bastard, to pay no attention to them and do what he wanted to do. I prefer to support him, rather than accuse him of being so rebellious in such a severe way. Apparently, the relationship is warm, really easy, but then, sometimes, I have the feeling that it is a cold, objectified relationship. I don't know how to explain it. I simply find it strange.

Agueda Segado: My experience with type VII has been basically in groups. In that situation I can see very well how they seduce, how they take control of the sessions, how they buy the others, etc. In groups, I have seen myself acting in two different ways. If they are involved, I have a gift for bringing them down from their fantasy and connecting them with pain, but if they are resistant, evasive, and acting the clown, I usually pay no attention and don't get involved in their games. I am even quite hard.

In individual therapy, although my experience is recent, I am usually warmer. I don't mind if they think they are in control of the session, that they are the ones to ask me first how I am, as if they were the therapist. It doesn't matter. It's a question of time for them to get down to business, although they don't do so directly. When I point out their games to them, I do it with tenderness.

Suzy Stroke: The challenge is their intellectual side. This I have to defeat in order to go over to trust, and from there silence their mental noise, give them my hand, and say: "Let's go as far as you can go. It's difficult, but I'm here to protect you. You can trust me." It is a matter of capturing their trust and also admiration. Then there is no chance of "escaping."

I do better with the women than with the men. The men require more attention for their innumerable traps, principally the seductive games in their many different forms.

Antonio Pacheco: I can remember the case of a type VII woman, very intelligent, skillful, and seductive. But her everyday life was a disaster in every respect: emotional, financial, professional . . . . She had that intellectual, idealistic side, making it difficult for her to face up to pain, to being a normal person. It seems like they are always above the rest in their world of evasion and dreams. It took her two years to begin to do something in her everyday life, to begin to put her feet on the ground.

My work with type VII is a continuous confrontation, although very delicate; a gentle fight and a lot of shelter and protection when they break down.

Riccardo Zerbetto: With type VII it's a difficult matter for me. They have a more natural contact with their own impulses and instincts, and type II is a little more restrained, less immediate. This can also be a useful element, because type VII is more of an amateur, more mobile, less serious, whereas type II is more serious about his or her affairs. It is not easy for type II to escape from the diagnosis of false self that type VII instinctively perceives: that is, where you are, your level of contact with yourself, your more spiritual level.

Paco Peñarrubia: It looks like it is difficult for everyone to work with type VII. Almost everybody agrees on that.

I corroborate the difficulty with type VII. It has taken me a great deal to learn to work well with them. To begin with, I felt that they were similar to me. In another period I couldn't stand them. I couldn't stand their softness, their weakness, their rebellion, their lack of discipline . . . . Now I feel fine with them and can work efficiently with their traps. It is as though I understood them well. I give support where it is needed, and I don't let them get away with anything when I observe their manipulations. What I like is that now I can do this without getting angry, without being more annoyed by their pathology than by others. I feel like a half-cured trickster who understands and denounces the black-marketeer he has before him.

THERAPEUTIC RELATIONS WITH TYPE VIII

Laura Martinez: Most of my type VIII patients have been children or adolescents. These are the people with whom I find it easiest to simply be myself, and not do anything.

Some months ago I was brought a little girl who had been labelled as "the little murderess." She was nine years old, and had tried to throw her younger brother off the porch. She had burned his hands with a blowtorch. She had tried to set fire to the house. She stole money—large sums, 10,000, 15,000 Ptas. [$100-$150]—from the family. She stole in school.

When the mother brought her (I think the mother was a type V), she ranted on about the child, explaining the things the little girl did, saying that she (the mother) didn't love her, that it was a shame she hadn't had an abortion . . . a somewhat complicated situation. The girl, meanwhile, looked at me, yawned and smiled, as if nothing were wrong. So I told the mother to bring the girl along for a couple of days, and I would have a look at her.

On the first day we went to the park. We picked up leaves from the ground and I would give her the leaf for her to find the matching tree. On the second day we went to a square to look at the pigeons and eat chocolate. Then I thought it might be a good idea to do something that might seem a little more therapeutic. So I said to her: "Look, let's sit down for a while and talk about this, about stealing and all that. Let's talk seriously, OK?" And she said yes.

We talked for a while. We both agreed that it was better not to steal, and then she started telling me about her mother, saying that she loved her a lot. We decided to get her mother a present. She said her mother really liked red flowers, so we bought her a little flower pot with a rosebush in it. The kid went down the street telling everybody: "It's for my mother! It's for my mother!" She was absolutely delighted. Nobody paid any attention to her, but anyway . . . .When her mother spotted us, she looked at us as if we were creatures from another world, as if she could not understand the business; she froze. From that day, the child was in therapy. She really surprised me too—I didn't expect the kid to stop stealing, to suddenly stop being a problem; but she did. It's really strange, I mean it seriously, I don't understand.

A few days before I came here, the mother came to see me. She was really happy, saying that she had a present for me. I think she is type V because the present she gave me was a roll of garbage bags and three kitchen cloths. She works as a cleaning-lady. She isn't educated and her language isn't good, but she was so excited. We kissed, and so forth . . . .

My other experience was with a type VIII group, a group of wild kids, thieves, who would fight. It was impossible to do anything with them, they were accomplices. I think that somehow what I do is enter into complicity with them. With these kids, I found it really hard to get them to brush their teeth and go to school and all those things. Once I left them alone for four days. I left two tutors in my place. When I got back they had stolen, they hadn't gone to school, they had fired small shot at my car, they had broken all the windows . . . a disaster. They said they were only checking if the windows were resistant to the small shot.

In general, my story has been being with them, loving them, defending them from the world (I believe type VIII are people who have never felt defended), and defending the world from them, so nothing should go wrong in the meantime.

Elena Revenga: I have little experience of a long process of therapy with type VIII. They bring out tenderness and complicity in me, in the initial contacts. I think a relationship with type VIII is an art—representing the law with tenderness and complicity at the same time.

Agueda Segado: My experience with type VIII has always been in groups. They bring out a lot of tenderness in me. Their innocence moves me. I only felt scared in one case. It was with a person to whom I was giving a lot of support. One day I saw his seduction—how he looked for my complicity. At the same time I also saw that he could kill me. That's where I felt afraid and became alert. Something like: "I'm not going to get involved in your game."

Suzy Stroke: The way in which I have managed to handle the people with this character is precisely with complicity, and with being able to walk together with them in that marginal world, which is how they come to you—causing an impact in order to frighten you. "Are you going to be able to understand me? Are you going to have the balls to put up with me?" Really, it requires walking with them without any fear. After that, a lot of physical contact and affection is essential. They do not know what it is to receive affection. But it really has to be genuine. If it isn't, if you are making a therapeutic manipulation, type VIII see this, and it's over. You have to genuinely feel, otherwise it doesn't work. Truth, face-to-face, is the basis of a relationship with type VIII.

Antonio Pacheco: My experience with type VIII was more with adolescents, in the days when I worked in schools. I remember working with a gang where the leader was type VIII. The meetings were a struggle for power, a continuous confrontation in order to put me to the test, as if intending to frighten me. They tested me several times, with the teachers and the students, to see if I respected their secrets and deserved their trust. In order to be able to work with them I became their confidant and accomplice. Finally, one day, the leader said to me in front of the gang: "I think we can trust you." He gave me 3,000 dollars they had stolen in a house, wanting me to change it into pesetas and split it with them. They wanted to turn me into a delinquent. I didn't manage to convince them to give the money back, because they held that the owner was rich, but I did manage to get them to agree to give the money to the poor, and that's what we did. It was moving to go out into the street with them and share the money among the beggars we found. I think they felt good and generous; they were happy. From that moment they trusted me and they improved a lot. The gang gradually broke up. Little by little they found jobs. Even now, eight years later, the leader comes to see me every now and then, when he has problems or difficulties. He is married and has a daughter.

I think that what helped in the relationship was complicity, maintaining authority, trust, and acceptance.

Riccardo Zerbetto: With type VIII there is a lot of conflict for me, although both types (II and VIII) are also complementary in the sense that type VIII is a seductive type . . . or rather, is into grabbing things. This is why there can be a good exchange, in the sense of a subtle form of conquest of type II. I don't have any examples. I'm saying this a bit like an hypothesis of what can happen as competition between the two of them, as regards the power involved in the therapeutic relationship.

Paco Peñarrubia: I hadn't worked with type VIII for years, but lately I have several. I realize that I work well with them.

Antonio mentioned complicity. I don't feel much like an accomplice of theirs. What I do feel is unconditional—I never get involved in judging what is happening to them. Instead, they bring out a loving attitude in me, and also the attitude of not letting them get away with anything. It is difficult until they respect me, but normally they respect me quickly. After that the relationship works pretty well.

Specific things: my work is usually based on accompanying them on the way to touching their vulnerability, their pain, their weakness, and not allowing avoidances. This is the most difficult part, but that's the way the work has to go. Immediately after that they try to kill me, cut my head off. This I also always translate for them, as if I were saying: "You're killing me, you're cutting my head off, because I have witnessed your weakness, and you need to kill the witness." And they say: "Yes, it's true." Everything is a tug-of-war between, "I'm here, you don't need to kill me," and, on the other hand, "You can open up, I'm not going to use it against you." I like them a lot as people, the way they are. They are good fun.

What I can't stand is when they come acting aggressively with things in their life, full of rage and vengeance. Then the adrenalin starts going up the walls of my office, and it finally suffocates me. I have to stop them in order to be able to breathe. Except in these adrenalin increases, I feel comfortable working with them.

THERAPEUTIC RELATIONS WITH TYPE IX

Elena Revenga: With type IX I feel as if I were sitting in my own living-room. It is a relationship with a lot of solidarity. When type IX turn up, they have my recognition of them as people. This will be maintained throughout the whole process. It is a recognition "simply because," as human beings. It is, "I'm with you. I care about you."

In the relationship a great deal of trust is established. The work is a continuous development of attention (internal and external), with tasks that are so simple that it is almost impossible not to do them.

With the sexual type IX's the process is more dynamic. (Perhaps they are the ones most ready for action.) The process amounts to realizing and changing things, almost immediately.

One thing I am generally careful about with type IX, in the three subtypes, is my use of criticism. Usually it is received as disparagement and devaluation, and normally leads to blocking. The relationship is made up of recognition-confrontation and explicit support.

Joan Garriga: I have a person who hasn't been in therapy for long. For me, on one hand, the most important thing has also been trying to put through this message of, "I'm interested in you; you interest me." On the other hand, in work itself, almost the only thing I have done is increase his power of discrimination a little. There is one side of this specific person that exasperates me—his literal, or very concrete thing. On the cognitive side, what I do is work on making concrete things a little more abstract, turning literal things into something a little more conceptual.

Ignacio Lopez: What I really like about type IX is their will, although at the moment in which they start coming to therapy many of them are addicted to action. I like working with them by taking advantage of this aptitude they have for action, and then helping them to develop attention, focusing their awareness on the things they do. I like that a lot.

Where they sometimes confuse me is when they sit there, quietly, and I wonder, "Well, what is happening to these guys?" I ask them, and they say: "No, nothing." And Elena says it's true, nothing *is* happening to them. This is a side of type IX that I find difficult to understand. On the other hand, they bring out an unconditional attitude in me. In fact, also on a personal level, there is something facilitating the link.

Annie Chevreaux: With type IX there are two parts for me. The first part of the process is an easy and satisfactory relationship. The trust they place in me moves me and makes me work at my ease. They surrender themselves a lot. They get involved, and then they are grateful, however little you help them. In that phase, in which they learn to take their place, to attack, to realize how they have allowed themselves to be exploited, a good relationship is created.

The difficulty comes later, when they have matured more, when they already know how to do it. I have a patient who has already finished her therapy who comes to me now and then to complain about her difficulties. She makes me responsible for the fact that things should be so hard (now that she is doing better than ever). I feel that she comes to whine. (Well, I see it as whining, from my type perspective, V). So the relationship cools off.

I feel happy when they enhance their awareness, but when they lose it and whine, that's where I close the door and withdraw. I find it hard to stay next to them in that phase.

Agueda Segado: With type IX, for me, the most important thing (and here I agree with Elena) is for them to feel appreciated and recognized as people. I believe that when they feel this the process works more quickly.

I also work a lot on "here and now," having them enhance their awareness of the present moment so they can get out of mechanical chatting and mechanical movements, which for me represent avoiding the experience of getting in touch with themselves.

One example which I find significant, of how type IX are distracted and also distract the therapist, occurred with a patient who quite frequently made pelvic movements during the session. One day, when I asked him what those movements meant to him and what was the use of them, it turned out that he was not aware of them. When the movement stopped he said: "If I stop making the movement, I don't exist before you."

My experience with type IX is that when they integrate their dark side: aggression, selfishness, cruelty . . . they stop a lot of behavior that used to be unconscious, both for themselves and for others.

For me, the most difficult thing in the process with type IX has been to discover that, when they are about to surrender themselves and trust the therapist, they make an unconscious effort to do what they consider to be seizing therapeutic control. For example, if they used to pay cash, they start paying with checks, or they come late. As soon as you bring the subject up, they say: "You aren't always going to be in charge." They are touchy people who suspect they are not going to be genuinely taken into consideration and appreciated.

Suzy Stroke: With me they find it easy to transfer. They also bring out my maternal side. My problem with them is not when they are quiet, it is when they begin to speak, linking one issue to another. They don't stop. The talk has nothing to with what is going on, it merely looks like a way to distract themselves and the therapist from the real issue. It irritates me a lot and I don't know what to do when they start these things. Once I decided to record a session (which lasted much longer than usual) until the patient got tired of talking. I finished the session by asking her to transcribe the tape, making notes of what might appear to be relevant. She came back feeling embarrassed, realizing, a little bit, how she was wasting her own and my time. Then we were able to work.

I also see a lot of slowness, that business of the type IX not being able to perceive what is going on. You have to explain the same thing a million times in a million different ways, even the simplest thing, until you get an "Oh, yes!" In my case, in which everything has to be fast and you can't lose time with nonsense, I end up exercising my patience, which doesn't do me any harm.

Antonio Pacheco: Well, I have little to add. I also get exasperated with that empty discourse, and that action, that is always evasive action. Sometimes it is a lot of chaotic activity in order to be in the clouds. In general they are good patients. They surrender themselves easily and are usually willing. The work is usually slow, like working with a child who has to be taught little by little. I have tried everything with them and they accept it. They are usually grateful, even though you only give them a little help. It is a matter of patience and of respecting their rhythm, although sometimes I find this difficult and I push them.

Riccardo Zerbetto: Type IX is one of the types who easily get involved with type II, because type II's vital, strong and confident side acts in a very seductive manner on type IX. It is also a question of type IX remaining with their own story, more in touch. So, this game doesn't work unless there is a deeper level of awareness.

Paco Peñarrubia: There also appears to be considerable agreement, that working with type IX is relatively easy work, with the difficulties of slowness, or mobilization, or insight. I have, more or less, the same feeling.

My experience with type IX is that they come and deposit themselves on me. Yes, just as it sounds: they deposit themselves on me. My whole task is giving back to them what they have deposited on me—above all, awareness. I believe that what they delegate to me is awareness. So, half the therapy with type IX is being their awareness, and the other half is for them to start being it themselves.

I like working with type IX because they surrender themselves. They are quite dedicated and they give you presents at Christmas.

Chapter 5

A GROUP INQUIRY INTO THE DYSFUNCTIONAL ASSUMPTIONS AND ADMONITIONS CHARACTERISTIC OF THE TWENTY-SEVEN INSTINCT-RELATED SUBTYPES

I. INTRODUCTION:

Claudio Naranjo: The report that follows could have been more simply entitled "Peeking At Unconscious Fantasy." It is the result of an exploration of implicit thought patterns that are intimately linked to our behavior—but thought patterns in which we "don't truly believe," and must admit that it would be more or less crazy to endorse. Thus the expression, "crazy ideas." During a symposium morning, my proposition, to the participants in the characterologically-homogeneous groupings, was to discuss their observations in regard to their more commonly observed "automatic thoughts" and underlying assumptions, particularly in relation to problematic situations. I also suggested that, should time permit, they consider what ways of thinking might be therapeutic to cultivate. (Not all found the necessary time to tackle this last issue in view of our tight schedule, however.)

The seating arrangement in the course of the plenary session, of which the text below is the transcript, was that of a ring, echoing the placement of personality styles in the Enneagram. As a microphone was passed along in the large room, it was taken, not only by people reporting on the conclusions gathered from the small group meetings, but by individuals who felt inclined to elaborate or add information, either as fellow group participants, or out of their own experience.

Just as I kept my comments to a minimum as facilitator during the plenary meeting of sharing, I have abstained from comment as this goes into writing, deeming the document, as it stands, to be of sufficient stimulus value to seekers and therapists alike.

II. REPORTS FROM THE GROUPS:

A. Type IV

1. Self-preservation IV's:

Reporter: The meeting that we self-preservation IV's had was very short, productive and fast. We were the first to go down for the coffee break, and when we were taking the sun, after the meeting, we began to feel that perhaps we had not worked with enough tenacity. But, overall, we were very satisfied. We made a thorough collection of our crazy ideas and later the sane, healthy thoughts or antidotes.

Crazy ideas:
- "If I enjoy myself, I feel threatened by death."
- "There's not enough in the present moment, but when I go to . . . , I'll be better."
- Negative Judgements: "I'm wrong." "I'm bad." "I'm fastidious."
- "It's never enough! If I'm not a '10,' I'm nothing."
- "My worth depends on what I do and achieve. If I don't do anything, I disappear."

- "I'm not worthy." "I won't be supported by the outside world." "It doesn't work."
- "If I don't do a lot of things well, then they won't know I'm here."
- "There is only one 'spot'; it's you or me."
- "If the outside doesn't notice me, then I am empty."
- "I am marvelous, or I am shit."
- "I punish myself because I am me."
- "In order to have, I must do things." "If I have it, I have to do things."
- "I'm not good enough to be lovable."

After this system of crazy ideas, the antidotes or sane ideas:
- "Confidence in my place."
- "Validation of each small step."
- "In the present and in myself there is enough."
- "I'm good at seeing what's wrong."
- "Take advantage of what I have right now."
- "Accept what I am."
- "I am worthwhile for who I am."
- "I give myself a little space to do nothing, to breathe."
- "I don't have to be special."
- "There is enough just being."
- "Let them love me 'just because.'"
- "Make friends with chaos and craziness."
- "A renouncing of change."
- "Little by little."

2. Social IV's:

Reporter: We of the social subtype group did not do the sane idea part; we stayed with the crazy ideas. There are a lot of them in relation to exposing ourselves.

Crazy ideas:
- "I don't have a right to expose myself."
- "Showing oneself is presumptuous."
- "Don't be yourself."

- "If I show myself, I hurt someone else."
- "Emotional intensity is necessary in order to get anything."
- "All or nothing, in friendship or in anything."
- "If they love *you* it's the same as that they love *me* less."
- "If I show my strength, they won't love me."
- "If I show that I am worthwhile, I am attacking others."
- "When someone else has merit, they are attacking me."
- "If I show how much I suffer, they are going to love me."
- "If I show weakness, they will reject me."
- "If I show my strength, I will feel accepted but not loved."
- "I am the good one. Not the others."
- "Don't expose yourself, they could find you out."
- "Don't expose yourself so as to avoid rivalry."
- "Lose so as to win later."
- "Seduce with kindness."
- "They'll get theirs!"
- "Here I'm not anybody, but up there . . . ."
- "They'll take me from the ashes, magically."
- "When I finally have it, affection is no longer worth anything."
- "If they come to me, why could it be?"
- "I exist when I am seen."
- "If you don't acknowledge me, then I am not worthwhile."
- "I possess an extremely special quality. Someday, someone very special will discover it."
- "Deep down, I am the woman."
- "Any difference is an aggression."
- "If I show my desire, they may see me as inadequate, stupid . . . ."
- "I am going to end up ridiculous. I don't measure up."
- "There's something bad in me."

- "If they haven't loved me, it's because I haven't deserved it."
- "Pleasure is something that I don't deserve."

3. Sexual IV's:

Reporter: Well, we sexual IV's also do not have any sane ideas. We have spent all of the session fighting among ourselves, looking to see which was *the* crazy idea. As if there were only one! Well, we have cried, laughed, etcetera, etcetera, very vehemently. There were, above all, two ideas that came into clear relief. One was, "This is paradise!" and the other was, "This is hell!"

Crazy ideas:

Having to do with, "This is paradise!":
- "Everything is fine. And given that, whatever is not okay infuriates me because it hurts." (It is like abso lute intolerance of the minimum frustration—waiting for the sun to enter in at that place where I want it to enter, and if it doesn't enter there, then it pisses me off.

Having to do with "This is Hell!":
- "I can't trust anyone."
- "Everything is bad."
- "No one can love me."
- "The flesh is weak."
- "They can promise you love, but in the end they will love someone else."
- "If I show love or affection, they'll betray me. Therefore, it's not good to show love because it causes harm." (This idea was very common.)

B. TYPE III

1. Social III's:

Reporter: Well, we social III's have also not been able to see the antidotes. Perhaps we extended ourselves, once having found the crazy ideas, toward searching out the origins, or what we had in common. In fact, listening to the other groups, we have seen that we shared all the crazy ideas. We have seen, perhaps, the nuances which were more present in one subtype than in another. So then, this is what we have come up with.

Crazy ideas:

- "If all the world were like us, there wouldn't exist any problems; there wouldn't be any problems."
- "As you are, no one is going to love you." (In almost everyone, or in many of the representatives of the group, that idea—"As you are, no one will love you"—had been echoed by someone in their family. Or, there was some hint of, "If you grow, no one is going to love you." That statement carried a connotation of infantileness which, in each case, led us to not show how we are. . . just in case. Because, "They won't love us as we are," right?)
- "I don't need anything." (This has seemed to us to be the result of the fact that when we needed something there wasn't anyone who was going to give it to us. So then, it was better not to need anything. That was the origin of having arrived at, "I don't need anything.")
- "Wanting is power." (In this crazy idea there is a second line of thought which would be, "One must be able to do all that one can." That is to say, on the one hand there is a very great confidence in everything that we want to accomplish, but to avoid failure we always want what we *know*, with certainty, we are going to be able to achieve.)
- "I will never be with a man for money. I will earn it myself and then I will choose for myself." (Here there have arisen different images of mothers who used their daughters to get money in a situation where there was total economic dependence on the father, or mothers who manipulated in order to obtain money directly from the father, again because of total economic

115

dependency on the father.)

- "If I get married, I will never separate." (Here we have verified that the majority of us is not married, and the ones who are married did so after much reflection and almost as a jump into the void. The problem is that, "If I once dare to give my affection to someone and this fails me, it would be the ultimate failure." It's a fear of the great failure.)

- "Everything that I want no one else will give to me, unless I accomplish it myself." (There is a shade of this that goes, "Life will give me nothing. I accomplish everything based on effort." That is to say, "Everything that I want I will get for myself, and moreover with effort." "Nothing will come to me as a gift.")

- "I *am* to the extent that I have worth, and not to the extent that I am."

And then, beneath all of these things that we have in common, which had led us to these crazy ideas, there was, therefore, a feeling of great emptiness. That is, a feeling of, "All these external things . . . but where are we?"

2. Self-preservation III's:

Reporter: In the self-preservation III group they were already taking notes before we all agreed. More concretely, there would be the following crazy ideas:

- "Be cheerful." (The crazy idea would be, "We don't have problems." A little bit like, "As we cannot have problems, well, we are cheerful.")

- "Find fast solutions for everything." (Here we have related it to the so-called "superficiality of the III" in the sense of not going deeply into things. It is also related to, "We don't have problems." Thus, for the littlest thing that breaks down: "Bam," a fast solution so as not to have that problem.

- Another very interesting crazy idea had to do with not recognizing the body's rhythm. The fundamental idea was: "My body is at my service like all other things." Therefore, we don't recognize tiredness or we don't recognize the rhythm or physical needs."

3. Sexual III's:

Reporter: With regard to the sexual III there are perhaps two crazy ideas that stand out:

- "You are not worthy. No one is going to love you." There was a background film of, "The fact is that you're not good enough to get married."
- And parallel to, "You're not good enough to get married," would be the crazy idea that, "I am worth a lot, but since I am not good enough to get married, I'm very good at driving a man mad for two days." (There is the need to be good for something, and in as much as I'm not good enough for marriage, then at least I'll drive someone crazy for a few days.)

We were commenting here also on the issue—

- "One has to be . . . like superwoman." (We also discussed an idea that it's like giving an image of a woman, but from the point of view of conduct. It's very masculine, because from the place of what is "typical feminine emotionality" it's difficult to connect. Above all, it's hard to receive affection from outside, even though that's what we want most.)

Contributor: I'm going to put the positive side in. Apart from the fact that I have obviously identified with all of the crazy ideas, what for me has been helpful has been to concretize within myself and see what has really given me the most, at least at this time in my life. It has been helpful to consider who can be my friends, or who are the people I love a lot. It hasn't taken a lot of effort, since they love me for what I am. It's as if I have counterbalanced my crazy idea that, "Through effort, etcetera, is how I will get affection, others' love." Because, if I really stop to be with myself, life itself demonstrates to me that they love me for what I am. Even though it's harder than anything for me to recognize it.

To not recognize the love of the other is to devalue the other, as if they don't have the capacity for choice or discretion. "The other knows what you are; you are not always fooling them. And, they love you for what you are also."

There are things that life gives you without effort, although it has been one of my maxims in life: "Everything is based on effort," but I know that's not true.

Contributor: Myself also, in relation to effort, I feel that: "Yes, everything I got was through effort," but what I feel has changed recently is the motivation for the effort. Efforting is there, it remains in me; but the motivation is now clearer to me, it's no longer so automatic. So, that allows for moments of more relaxation. Also, I relate to the idea: "I trust that I don't have to control everything, that there is something that controls better than me."

C. TYPE II

1. Sexual II's:

Reporter: Contrary to what normally occurs in the type II group where there is general disagreement, where everybody says everything at once, and where there is an impressive amount of gibberish, on this occasion there has been an incredible amount of agreement—unanimity in practically everything that came up. It has seemed to us especially productive. It has amazed us to see so much affinity in the things that we discussed, and so much internal resonance with what we were hearing from each other. Having thought that, ". . .this could not have occurred to anyone except me," but then to hear it from others in exactly the same way has been a great surprise. With regard to the crazy ideas, we connected to:

> - "The effort to please everyone," or especially, to please certain people. (This leads us into great difficulty when it's time to take in criticism. A very big problem, when something goes wrong, is having to accept

rejection or invalidation. It is like there is an internal fear of the possibility that others may see inside us, the feeling of being found out "for who I am," the suspicion that really, behind it all, well, "I'm nothing," right?)
- The interpretation of criticism as synonymous with, "They don't love me." "If they criticize me, it means that they don't love me."
- Being very demanding with oneself. "I can do every thing," or also, "I know everything."
- "If they fall in love with me it's because they love me." (That is, an identification of sexuality or attraction with love. That attraction is the confirmation that one is marvelous—that one is loved.)

With regard to the sane ideas, there have been a lot that are all along the same lines:
- "Acceptance of one's faults and one's lacks."
- "Others have the same rights as me."
- "Become conscious of one's needs."
- "I'm like everyone else, one more."
- "I can't do everything. Things are hard for me."
- "Don't try to be marvelous so that others will love or accept me."
- "Love is not something that is bought and sold. It's something that is given." (That attitude of obtaining love voluntarily.)
- The idea that, "I can owe something to others."
- The idea of, "Accepting one's weakness and manifest- ing it. That a II's weakness be seen." (In contrast to the II's crazy idea that, "Our weakness and our failures must not be seen."

2. Social II's:

Reporter: We were looking at it, perhaps, through the rela- tionship with the father. It's different the way the male social type II tries to reach his father from the way a woman can reach him.

Above all, the group provided the enjoyment of finding ourselves and discovering other similar people for the first time, because for the majority of us it was the first time we had such a discussion. But there's no report or summary.

Claudio: But, I assume that the specific crazy idea of a confusion of love with admiration, was discussed. An interpretation of how the desire to be loved somehow is transformed into this desire?

Reporter: Of course. We discussed how we are dominated most by this position of being on top as a way of managing to be loved.

3. Self-Preservation II's:

Reporter: Well, in the self-preservation group not many crazy ideas have come out, but a few healing ideas have, like:
- "Our needs are not so great."
- "We can find satisfaction in simple things."
- "Express rage and displeasure in the face of frustration."
- "Don't control, and don't control oneself in relationship."
- "Allow the little girl side to show; it's really okay."

Claudio: Is there some kind of crazy idea that one has to continue on in life being a child? Because sometimes it has been said, even in official psychology, dynamic psychology, that one of the labels that exists is that of the infantile character. It took me a long time to realize that what was being called an infantile character was the self-preservation II. And, I imagine that it is an alternative to sexual seduction. It's not that it's incompatible, but that it's a seduction from the position of the child. As if there exists, like a maternal-paternal impulse in everything, a kind of seduction that is specialized. So it's like a difficulty in growing up. I don't know if it came up. Was the crazy idea spoken of as if one must continue?

Reporter: It wasn't discussed. What we have talked about is that as children we didn't permit ourselves the role of little girl. It's like we were children who quickly became adults.

Claudio: The internal perception doesn't coincide with the external perception I think. Do you feel like someone who didn't have a childhood, who grew up too fast and became a man?

Reporter: I feel that when I was a child I tried to look like a grown up person.

Claudio: And now you are divorcing?

D. TYPE I

1. Self-Preservation I's:

Reporter: We are the self-preservation I group—worry. We only had enough time to look at the stains, the crazy thoughts.

- The first that came up was, "Don't ask for anything." (That is, not asking for anything is surrounded by a whole slew of crazy ideas: "Don't ask, because if they give you anything you'll have to reciprocate. But if they don't give to you, you'll be frustrated and you won't be able to stand the suffering." "Don't ask for anything because if they give it to you and you like it you'll be dependent." All having to do with that script about not asking for anything.)
- Then, as if through that previous idea, one can deduce, "Figure it out for yourself," "Be autonomous," "Be in dependent," "Don't depend on anyone." The issue goes on like that.
- Then there was, to some extent, an underlying idea like: "We don't matter to anyone," "Deep down everyone forgets about me," or something like that. "There isn't any help for me."
- Another belief: "People don't get close to us because they love us, but because we give to them." And from that comes the belief that, "I have to give a lot so that, in that way, others will love me," "I have to do a lot of things and do them very well so that I can in that way obtain affection."
- And the negative part would come from the belief that, "I don't deserve it," because deep down there is

121

such low self-esteem. And together with that idea there would be a "fear of punishment." Fear of permanent punishment, that is to say, the punishment could be that they don't approve of me, that they don't love me, that they don't value me, etcetera.

- The fear of punishment also motivates us to overwork at doing everything well; so from that, "I have to work hard, try hard," "I have to worry about everything working out properly, because if I don't do it, they won't love me." Or, even worse, "They will punish me." (I sometimes think that when I do something I'll be happy if they at least don't punish me. That's enough for me to be satisfied.)

- We spoke a bit about sexuality and desire in terms of "denying need," even more strongly than the type II. That is, to harden oneself so as not to feel need as a way of not suffering. Tied, perhaps, to that script of not asking for anything. "If I don't feel needs, I don't have to ask, and in that way I can take care of things my self."

I think these were the essential points.

2. Sexual I's:

Reporter: Those of us in the sexual type I group also only got as far as formulating the crazy ideas:

- "Whatever I don't control, I lose."
- "I must answer to the expectations of others to be loved."
- "I don't ask for anything so as not to show my need."
- "I am not sufficiently excellent or perfect."
- "No matter what I do, it's never going to be good enough."

Claudio: Aren't there any rigid people in this community? I see . . . . Oh! They are all taking a break.

E. TYPE IX

1. Sexual IX's:

Reporter: We didn't get to the curative ideas either. Here are the crazy ideas:

- "When we don't want to see or acknowledge something about ourselves, and someone tells us, we experience it as an attack and we defend ourselves."
- "I have to give in to keep them by my side."
- "I have to keep the peace at all costs."
- "If I express my need, they won't love me."
- "I don't have the right to ask for anything."
- "If I don't say something interesting they won't pay attention to me and I don't have anything interesting to say."
- "If you don't look at me and pay attention to me, you don't love me and I'm not taken into account or I'm not present. I'm not valued."
- "If I do what I need to do, something horrible is going to happen." (It's like not disturbing the established order.)
- "If I ask for anything, I'm bothering."
- "If they criticize me, they disqualify me." (A feeling as if they destroy us.)
- "If they criticize me, I punish them with indifference."
- "They'll never give me back as much as I give."
- "We are right."

2. Self-Preservation IX's:

Reporter: When we began we got a little lost. We put together a list first and then we realized that we had made a mistake and we had to put together another. The truth is that the first time around we had a very good time, we laughed a lot, and I'll read it later. But first I'll read what we put together the second time around:

- "No one perceives my needs."
- "I'm my father's special little girl, always, and he will take me into account."
- "I have to be serious for them to love me."
- "I shouldn't bother anyone or others."
- "No one recognizes me."
- "I'm not sexually attractive to anyone."
- "I'm nothing and I don't have a place in the world."
- "I mustn't do ugly things."
- "I shouldn't or I can't feel desires."
- "I shouldn't provoke anyone."
- "I can't show what I want."

I'd say that the common tone of the self-preservation IX group is that we desire. There is a kind of desire or crazy idea that others love us without our having to give ourselves over to it before hand. That is, that they should love us for ourselves alone. This doesn't mean that we are unable to love; we are capable of loving but we want to be loved by others in this sense.

And then, the list we put together in the first place, when we laughed a lot, says more or less the following:

I want:

- "That everyone else know my wishes and accommodate them without any effort on my part."
- "That my father consider me his special little girl and that he take that into account."
- "To be able to externalize happiness or an internal boisterous frolic."
- "Not to think that I could bother anyone."
- "That there is a recognition, dedication, and devotion by everyone else toward me."
- "To be able to externalize my sexual appetite."
- "To differentiate my individual part from what pertains to everyone else, and to form part of and feel a part of the world."

- "To be able to experience myself without depending on everyone else."
- "To be able to please a harem of women or men, enjoying myself without the least effort."
- "To be able to feel desire for whatever arises."
- "To dance the dance of the seven veils."
- "To be able to evoke lusty passions in others."
- "To be able to punish women or men so as to find my rightful place."

Nothing more.

3. Social IX's:

Reporter: We social IX's have made a very short list because there was no consensus. One of us changed over to the sexual IX group, and two more of us don't any longer know whether we are social or sexual IX's. So the crazy ideas that have come out are:

- "Adapt myself because I can't do anything."
- An idea of impotence: "As I won't be able to change anything, I'll let myself go along. It's not worth the effort."
- "In the face of confrontation, indifference. That's where strength lies; that's the weapon of power."
- "If I confront, I'll end up alone."
- "Not expressing my own ideas for fear of exposing my self, because what's mine has no value."
- "I don't believe in my ideas, in what I'm worth."
- "What comes from others is more comfortable."

And that's as far as we got.

F. TYPE VIII:

1. Sexual VIII's:

Reporter: We VIII's, I think, continue to be in our natural rebellion and anarchy. Nothing! We have done hardly anything! We've gone to the bar; we've smoked; we've drunk coffee. Let's see; we were, in this group, three sexual VIII women, and one to whom we have been dedicating a lot of time because she's in that state of, "Do I belong with the VIII's?" We discussed, "Is she in, or is she out?; Does she live it or doesn't she?" We dedicated a lot of time to relating things, to see if she could connect with us, to see that what she thought didn't connect, we thought was fundamental.

We have a couple of crazy phrases. I have one that goes:

- "I'm always going to leave." In my life this has meant (and I suppose also in the lives of my sexual VIII companions) movement. Difficulty in giving myself over to things and being enormously indifferent to others. The sane phrase would be, "I'm going to stay." And staying, staying still, produces a richness, a lot of restlessness, a lot of emptiness, but a lot of richness. To stop definitely, to stop. For us, at least for us sexual VIII's, to stop is fundamental for healing.

- Another phrase from another one of us was, "The world is dangerous." Some of us have children, and I personally said how I taught my daughters, "Never trust anyone, not ever, not anyone. Be alert, one must be prepared, they're going to trick you. This world is a business: they won't give to you unless you give, they won't give to you unless you work." And the clean phrase was, "Look cleanly upon the world, look upon it cleanly."

Claudio: Look cleanly upon the unclean world.

Reporter: And then there is a phrase from someone else, for which we haven't found the healthy side. She argued, and we argued, about relating or not relating, or how we are in the face of authority. She went back and forth between no . . . , yes . . . , that we who are the authority don't even bother to fight. And she has said, "No, no, no, I don't have the same idea as the rest of you. "For me power '*me refanfinfla.*'" (It has seemed to me a lapidary phrase, and for that reason I'm including it.) She's in doubt as to whether she's an VIII, she told us. That's it.

2. Self-Preservation VIII's:

Reporter: There are very few of us self-preservation VIII's, so here are our crazy ideas:
- "If they don't give me what I want, I get angry."
- A very typical one: "I'm not here, I'm not here." Right? "When something isn't interesting, I'm not here." (It's like withdrawing to satisfy my desire as soon as possible.)
- "One must go through life controlling things."
- "One cannot walk relaxed in the street."
- "One must be astute."
- "I am anesthetized."
- "One must capture others' attention, the more the better."
- "One only feels if the situation is on the edge."
- "When I want to change, I'll change."

I think it's good.

Claudio: I suppose you found yourselves to be Machiavellian . . . .?

Reporter: I haven't said that. "Subtle sadism toward people closest to us" is better.

Claudio: No, I think of it in the sense of an ideology in which the end justifies the means.

Reporter: The crazy idea is, "At least Napoleon or Hitler: whatever it takes to get there."

Claudio: "Whatever it takes to get there!"

Reporter: Fall whoever may fall! But at least Napoleon or Hitler, minimum. What's happening is that we're changing over to the good, right?

Claudio: You're becoming dangerously good.

3. Social VIII's:

Reporter: Well, we social VIII's have not managed to meet. One went to sleep, another one isn't here, a third one arrived a little late and was talking to two sexual VIII's and didn't pay any attention to us. In the end we didn't do anything. As a crazy idea, one of mine, if it's worth it, there's the idea that:

> - "If I love, I weaken myself." (It's not so much if I dare
>   to express it, as, if I dare to feel love, I become weak.)
>   And the positive idea, is the contrary: "Dare to feel, to
>   be weak, to allow myself to be how I am."

Claudio: I don't know if anyone has heard me tell about the
giant, in the story of Pinocchio—the one who puts Pinocchio in a
cage. He's an archetypical VIII, a kind of ogre. The story says
that every time he felt compassion he sneezed—a somatization to
protect himself. How can one go around armored in the world?
How can one triumph and play the strong one if one is susceptible
to this weakness called compassion? So then, it's one of the characteristics: "When his heart began to soften, he would sneeze and
that would interrupt it."

Contributor: There was a meeting of social VIII's that two
of us have gone to. It was a small meeting, but what we talked
about as one of our crazy ideas was:

> - "Look for tender people." (And one of us didn't find
>   one. But I have always gotten together with sexual II's.
>   All of the partners I have ever had, throughout my life,
>   were sexual II's. We were talking about that because it
>   was what we were interested in.)

G. TYPE VII

1. Social VII's:

Reporter: In the meeting of social VII's we had both social
and self-preservation VII's. Some of the ideas are:

> - "The more I give, or the more I'm given to, the more I
>   mistrust."
> - "If I give, they won't attack me."
> - "If I'm not useful, they won't love me." (There were a
>   lot of ideas like this, with a utilitarian vision of exist-
>   ence, like: "I come to the world with a mission and if I
>   don't accomplish it, I don't exist." Whatever the mis-
>   sion might be: for the parents, or making my mother
>   feel that she is a good mother, or making her feel that

we men are to be trusted. Any mission; but if I don't accomplish it, existence doesn't have a meaning.)
- This is more from the self-preservation VII's. They said: "Anything for them to love me! To be good or even to be bad, so long as they love me."
- "If I don't do things, I don't exist." (It comes from the same thing.)
- "I have more to do so that they will love me." (There the feeling of not being enough.)
- One area where there was differences was about the vision of the world. For some, "The world is painful so I avoid it"; and for others, "The world isn't painful, and if someone hurts it's because they set it up badly." (But we didn't really know if the world is painful and one mustn't look at it, or if it's Eden and the exceptions are painful. We were not very much in agreement on this. There are some of us who see it more one way than the other.)
- Also, between men and women there was a difference. There was an idea among the men that, "I have to be good for Mom," and among the girls it was "for Daddy," although there was also a man who coincided with this. For the majority it was "for Daddy" or "for Mom" depending on one's sex.
- Another idea is the lack of time: "There isn't time for us," "We have to run along," "Do it in a hurry," "Speak fast." (The feeling that there isn't time, related to some experiences, they said, in childhood where there was so little space that the little bit had to be taken advantage of. Therefore, "If you didn't say everything very fast, then there was no longer enough time left for them to listen to you," or something like that, right?)
- In relation to this, we discussed whether the world is black or rose-colored. Some people said that deep down there is a feeling that a catastrophe is going to happen, and in reaction to that comes the crazy idea of,

"Nothing's going on, everything is just fine," but very much with the feeling of a catastrophe in the background. (This was more from the side of the self-preservation VII's.)

- Many crazy ideas about, "One must be good above all." (Basically that message, and then, for when we aren't good, of course, it's all in always having an alibi or a justification. That is, that what's bad is not doing something bad, but rather, not having an adequate response if they catch you—not having an alibi, a justification, in case they catch you in it. Basically, we haven't talked about sane ideas. We made it this far with this.

2. Sexual VII's:

Reporter: Well, among the sexual VII's the first thing that we really noticed is that we didn't have permissive parents. Instead, it's as if they had imposed sobriety on us obligatorily.

- The parents say, "Don't be a capricious child," or some thing about sobriety as something obligatory.
- Also, among the women they said that: "You don't need anything if you do what I tell you."
- And in the face of this we developed, on the one hand, a rebelliousness, like a revenge: "I am going to have it all," "I don't need anything from you, I'm not going to ask you for anything," "I have no need of the other, the other needs me," "I deserve it," and also, "If you say 'no' to me, you don't love me."
- And, there is also another part, like a background of guilt in which one says to oneself: "I've done some thing wrong," "I've made a trap for myself," "I should admit my trick," "It's wrong to please oneself," and "They'll say 'no' if I ask for it directly." For this reason one also develops the strategy for obtaining what one wants from the other.

- There were differences between the men and the women. The women had a permissive father. With the men, the one who was permissive, above all, was the mother. The father was more spartan.
- There was also another type of idea that went like this: "Live and let live," "You have to figure it out for your self." Also, a feeling or an idea like, "Grow up fast to leave home."
- And a very deep, underlying idea that says, "I can't give in to pain because no one will take me out of it. I'll have to do it by myself," right? "No one's going to take care of me."

And there is also, as Paco (Paco Peñarrubia) has said, one thing which we don't know . . . . We have spoken little about it, but it's like a lost paradise or a living in paradise. Several of us had a traumatic experience very early in our childhood and we remember what came before this trauma as being a very happy childhood, very joyful, very fortunate. So we have the idea that paradise on earth still exists, as if we still have paradise, a lost paradise. I don't know very well how to say it.

Claudio: I feel tempted to ask something. I have encountered some VII's lately whose experience is not so much of a paradise lost, but of a very painful childhood. And I didn't know about that. It's as if there is a crazy idea that suffering is more catastrophic for other people, as if one has to take extra precautions to protect oneself from suffering because there is so much catastrophe associated with the idea of suffering.

Reporter: We discussed how, in the relationship with the parents, they demonstrated their love to us but they never told us they loved us. It was as if, "No feelings," although things are done, demonstrated, there is touch. But something that isn't present is *saying*, "I love you." Then, there is all that about the traumatic experience, having awareness of the pain, and of having felt very much alone, and abandoned. That has also come out. It's as if, at some moment, something had broken and . . . .

Claudio: As if optimism, like a hypomanic, for a defense against the depressive background.

131

H. TYPE VI

1. Social VI's:

Reporter: Well, in the social VI group we began with, "I can do everything." But we didn't like it very much. So, finally, we ended up with the crazy idea that we all liked which is:

- "I should be able to do everything."
- Also, "When things are far away, the feeling is one of omnipotence with everything; and when things are close," we say, "Oh my impotence,"— the contrary.
- "The next time I won't make it."
- "I follow the rules, but one day I'm going to get it."
- "If I don't do what I should, they won't love me."
- "If I do what I should, they will love me." (It came out both ways.)

Then there were two ways of living out the "rule" thing. There were some with a very submissive aspect—there isn't any questioning of the rules. Others always question the rules, but they'll follow them. What was clear was that one couldn't function independently of the rules, and the crazy ideas came out that:

- "One had to judge the one who didn't follow the rules or even shoot them." (Laughter.)
- "If I show my anger, I don't know what will happen, certainly a catastrophe."
- "If I let myself go, I'm going to kill someone."
- There was a tendency to always create discord and to provoke discussions, but when things reached a very aggressive point to stop. But then the tendency was to say, "I haven't done anything," yet to constantly be insidious, a pestering taleteller.
- "Obligation comes before devotion."
- "Any decision that is definite, any commitment is terrible."
- "Every gift is suspect. One cannot trust because what will I have to give in return for it later?"

And in the way of corrective thoughts, instead of, "I should be able to do everything" there were:
- "I have limits."
- What first came up was: "I *have* to say No," which was a rule again, and would really be, "I *can* say *No.*"
- Something else also came up, but we didn't concretize it too much. "Satisfy the inner desire more than the rules." We all agreed that if we could satisfy our wishes before we followed the rules, we would be much better.

Claudio: Which would be the idea to support that?

Reporter: I don't know.

Claudio: Something like, pleasure is worthwhile, or pleasure is as worthwhile as duty, I'd say.

Reporter: Yes. The way we observe that is very much in the opposite position—that obligation comes before devotion.

Claudio: I'm surprised that the type of person who is so pensive has produced a report that was not so formulated at the level of ideas as others. It's more like, "We're like this . . . " or, "We're like that . . . ." But they're not, at least in the way they were put into words, presented as ideas, crazy ideas.

2. Self-Preservation VI's:

Reporter: Among the self-preservation VI's we found, by a significant majority, almost unanimously, a high coincidence in what is happening deep down, or in the crazy ideas underlying different formulations. The incidences are in the kinds of conditional crazy ideas that go like this:
- "If I expose myself, they'll attack me, they'll disapprove of me, they won't love me." (That is to say, "If I expose myself, if I expose my authentic self, it's very dangerous.")
- "Outside there isn't any room for me, they are going to reject me, etc.."

- And the formulations can be, "If I expose myself, they'll attack me, or disapprove, therefore I shun exposing myself."
- "If I say No, they won't appreciate me. Therefore, I have to be agreeable, pleasant." (It's an adaptation out of necessity.)
- "The less I bother, the more affection I'll receive."
- "It's better not to say, so as not to make a mistake."
- "If I am self-centered and I fight for what's mine, they won't love me."
- "If I show my weakness or my incapacity, if I make a mistake, they won't love me."
- "If I don't do it right, they'll kill me."
- "If I show what I want, I will be betrayed."
- "If I am bad, aggressive, and I commit myself—that is, I expose myself as me—I won't be accepted. I'll end up alone."
- "If I get in touch with my pain, they'll see me as weak and so then they'll also reject me."
- "If I'm not sufficiently capable, intelligent . . . ." In the end it's all like that.
- "If I show myself as weak, they'll squash me."
- Underneath all this there is an awareness of lack of worth: "I'm not worth enough," "I am deeply unworthy, so I have to make a big effort."
- "I have to try hard to do what they ask of me."
- "I have to try hard for them to love me, but without exposing myself." (Thus, there is this awareness of lack of worth inside and the need to adapt to everyone else, fundamentally so that they will love me. It is interesting that not a single reference to the rules appeared. It was always an adaptation to everyone else, but as something human that would receive me, take me in.)
- "If I expose myself, I'll fuck it up."
- "If I show my hatred, I'll fuck it up."

- "If I don't confront, it'll go well for me." (Thus, this leads to the inhibition of action, at least one's own action, and taking refuge in thought. In thoughts, that is where one can develop the proper specificity, and on the other hand, beneath that great obligatory adaptation we were also aware that there was a great amount of inhibited aggression that could leap out, that was wanting to leap out to recover that which is one's own, that capacity to be one's self.)
- "I am guilty of hating, consequently I'll stuff my hatred." (And there was more in this direction.)

Corrective ideas for all of this? Being able to expose feelings and impulses.
- "I am worthy for what I am."
- Also, "I don't need everyone to love me in order to exist."
- "I am lovable just as I am, for myself, without having to do or fear anything."
- It would also be helpful, in this sense, to acknowledge that, "I don't love everybody."
- "I can show my weakness; I can expose everything that I repress."
- "I have the right to feel and show myself."
- "I show myself as I am, whether they like me or not."
- Also, "The fact that they don't love me doesn't mean that they are attacking me."
- And there is one that is even more radical: "I can change my mind whenever I want without it being a problem."
- A formulation that came up was: "To be able to break the good *and* the bad," where the imposed good is dependent on the established norm in the group, but not in the sense of a rule. That is, to be able to break the adaptation to, the fusion with, that good. And to break with the bad, where the bad is (as seen from our position) daring to be oneself. To break that law of what's good and what's bad.

Claudio: While you were speaking about that idea of incompleteness, that something is missing, I remembered a cartoon of a psychoanalyst who is speaking with a person who has no arms or legs, who is almost a cube with a head. And the analyst says: "I would say that your feeling of incompleteness comes from your oedipal situation in which your father . . . ." (Laughter.) I have the impression that all of those things that are difficult to expose, or of all the things that produce that feeling of incompleteness, aggression is the most fundamental. That what makes one so soft, what makes one so conciliatory, so much in need of affection and support, is that the person doesn't have the possibility to use his or her aggression because there is a crazy idea with regard to that.

Reporter: Yes, yes, absolutely.

Claudio: "That we must pacify ourselves," in the same way as the knight errants of the past, who would take off their helmets to show that they were not on the attack. I understand that it's the origin of the custom of taking off one's hat when greeting. It's as if that exaggerated, or contained, the showing oneself to be unarmed, defenseless.

A Question: . . . .

Claudio: Often IV's feel like VI's and VI's feel like IV's because the need for affection makes both melancholy. In the end, emotional dependence and suffering are tied together.

Question: What is the difference?

Claudio: The self-preservation VI is more into protection, into self-preservation; the social VI is more into being seen, the social domain is more developed, being before the world. Moreover, they (the social VI) are more ashamed; ashamed in the face of the world, in relation to stereotypical things. They are more refined, as if they were stretching themselves in order to be a not-so-aesthetic ideal. The aesthetic is very much linked to the ideal of the self.

Contributor: Last night, when we were coming back from the theater, that is precisely the same thing I had been commenting on with a social IV, because I had the feeling yesterday, when I was listening to them, that they had that point in common with us—a lack of a feeling of worth within ourselves. We found the difference, that while the social IV is more of a complainer from the side of feeling the lack of something that he/she doesn't have and that he/she demands, I think that with the VI's there isn't so much that emotional aspect as much as the need to adapt ourselves. That is, we lose ourselves there in the actions, more along the lines of a dissolution of our position, but with the aggression hidden inside, covered up by the complacency. The IV would be more likely to put on an ugly face because of what's not given to him/her, or because of what is missing, or because of what he/she doesn't dare do. In us, the VI's, that wouldn't be so noticeable. I believe that the shame is much more hidden.

Claudio: We've reached the strength VI's.

3. Sexual VI's:

Reporter: I wasn't aware that I was giving the report, and that's why I only wrote down the sane thoughts. (Laughter). I'll say it:

- "Trust in what's simple."

Claudio: Trust in what's simple.

Reporter: Yes. "Trust in love and . . . trust in love and abide." That is, in the face of the threat of abandonment, or the threat that something is going to happen, we will stop (a little) the impulse to chop heads off, the impulse to shift into aggression. That is, to stop the compulsive desire to escape and to chop off heads; rather, to believe in love.

Other sane ideas:

- "Remain."
- "Express my situation, whatever it may be."
- "Relate equal to equal."
- "Be sincere with others."
- "Renounce the kamikaze attitude."
- "Acknowledge fear."
- There was a person who said, "I move toward the bull to confront the bull, or I run in front of the bull." (It would be to stay, remain.)

- "Accept that there is a possibility of catastrophe, that anyway I can't stop all the catastrophes."
- "I'm not omnipotent."
- "In the face of aggression and feeling persecuted, to realize that I am the persecutor. To stay, remain."
- "Not to let go my aggression compulsively."
- "There is a lack of worth to withstand an intermediary situation."
- "To be able to be with anxiety."
- "In the face of absolute mistrust, to live inside the mistrust."
- "The courage to do things without confidence and without anyone's help."
- "To be as one is, strong and weak."
- "*All or nothing, better than or less than*, comes from a person who, in relation to others, is always vigilant of hierarchies, never coming from the position of equals to equals."
- "Because one cannot take anxiety, I act before I think. If you remained, stay with it. You see that you are able to."

Claudio: You already have resolved the thoughts. Good intentions are not lacking.

Contributor: We haven't written down the crazy ideas. It's a shame, because it's very useful. What I would like to say is that it seemed to me that the attitude common to all was the kamikaze attitude. That kamikaze attitude would be the impossibility of not being able to resist a confrontation—a need to confront without wasting time, because time during which we await a confrontation is torturous, or seems to be a torture. That is something very important. In the moment that one doesn't allow oneself to be taken over by the prejudice of, "I can't not confront," what happens is that one simply feels the anxiety. That is, one doesn't feel a terrible fear, it's simply anxiety. In addition, with time and with making a habit of listening to the anxiety, little by little the anxiety disappears by itself and courage comes out of that same anxiety. In this way, the issue that seemed to me to be common to all of us was to stop being pushed by anxiety, to endure the anxiety, and out of the anxiety allow courage to arise. Naturally, that means to resign oneself to the reality that one cannot take care of everything, one cannot resolve everything, and that, if a catastrophe has to take place, then it just takes place. There is not the possibility of defending oneself from everything.

I. TYPE V

1. Sexual V's:

Reporter: The sexual fives' crazy ideas are:
- "When I expose myself, I feel guilty."
- "I may have done it wrong. I will be forgiven everything."
- "If I say what I think, it's dangerous," or something like that.
- "What I think isn't worth the bother."
- "If I am too pleasant, or if I'm too seductive, that will obligate me, because then will come the contact, which is good, but if something more comes, bad!"
- "If I do it well or I show what I'm worth, later they'll demand it and I'll have to give an arm and a leg; so I don't do anything or I don't demonstrate."
- "If this one or that one abandons me, I'll find another. He/she loses out. I can go it alone. I can take anything."
- "I don't need to take care of myself physically: don't have to eat, don't have to indulge myself . . . ."
- "Without doing anything, they love me. That is, I don't have to do anything, I don't have to give anything."
- Then with the therapeutic relationship a polarity arises, which is a thought, "I know more about myself than he/she does." (That is, there is a mistrust, and then a surrender that comes from affection, a very great need of affection. Then comes devotion, or something like that.)

- "I am treated unjustly."
- "If I'm not in love, I don't feel like doing anything. I have no energy." So, there is a need for that, as if it gives the energy.

2. Self-Preservation V's:

Reporter: Among the self-preservation V's there wasn't anyone who made up a summary of our meeting. I'll read the notes that I took and perhaps one of my companions can add to it. With regard to the crazy ideas there were:

- "I wouldn't want to be devoured, but if I let myself, I'll be devoured."
- I wrote down, at a certain moment, a phrase from Groucho Marx which is: "I am alone so I am smart as no other." (Laughter)

Claudio: Repeat it, repeat it.

Reporter: "I am alone, therefore I am ready as I alone." (Laughter). In addition, this phrase has an advantage. I feel it to be very much V, in the sense that, changing one adjective, one can say many things: "I am alone, therefore I am attractive as I alone," etc. (Laughter).

- Another crazy idea is: "If I move, they know I'm here. If I don't move, they know I'm here." (Laughter). (I relate this a lot to the protagonist in Kafka's, *The Metamorphosis*. It is a little bit as if all the members of the body, and everything, were in disequilibrium which, in addition to transforming itself, transforms the environment. It's like an error from inside where you are. As if you didn't know what to do with the body and you were ashamed of it.)

With regard to sane ideas I also noted one which seemed very important to me:

- "To let oneself loosen up, to know how to accept and live with the great confusion of feelings and emotions," which is for us the counterpart to intellectual control. In emotions and feelings there is a great dearth of points of reference, and we don't know what to do with them. (A lot of laughter and applause.)

3. Social V's:

Reporter: Well, it seems like there aren't anymore commentaries from the V's.

Contributor: There is a commentary which I think is shared, as much in the social as in the self-preservation V's, as we were speaking together. It's something like:

> - "If I open my heart completely to the person I love, they are not going to love me." (That was something that was very common, because, "I don't have the right to be loved.")

Contributor: Now I have finally dared to come out a little better. The commentary that has seemed important to me has been how we have experienced a very strong emotional confusion. I have experienced this with my mother—like not knowing what was the role I was being asked to play, from when I was very small. Then it's as if I lived through a great emotional confusion—and that's what one wants to avoid, if one enters into emotion. (It would be like what is phobic and feared.) To feel emotions one must also become confused, but that is characteristic of emotional life, and it's not a problem.

Claudio: And how was the meeting? Was it interesting among yourselves?

Reporter: It was very emotional. (Laughter.) I experienced it like that. There was only one of us who didn't speak. We would say to her that it was all right to talk, and she said that it was good for her to listen. We were very united, and moreover, it was discussed that one of us was in love, and it was very important.

Chapter 6

NINE INGREDIENTS FOR A PANACEA

by CLAUDIO NARANJO, M.D.

We know that understanding is the distinguishing characteristic of the more experienced and successful psychotherapists of all schools, and that, in addition to understanding, a therapist's "bag of tricks" also counts: the sum of techniques, strategies and theories constituting professional culture and education. Beyond these, there is a relational and infectious element in psychotherapy too, that some today value even more than theory and technique: a willingness to *be for* the other, and, along with the capacity for benevolence, a degree of emotional and spiritual health on the part of the therapist that may only be attained through a relative transcendence of the personal neurosis in the course of a deep therapeutic process.

Aside from these universal ingredients of psychotherapy, there are others that, universal as they may be, seem to fit the needs of a particular kind of personality most specifically.

An ennead of these will be the subject of these paragraphs.

Let us begin with therapeutic insight. Insight is the designated task of many therapists, and a vehicle for all kinds of passengers. But, it is most fitting in the case of a pathology at the heart of which lies a sort of psychological deadness—a lack of psychological mindedness—in the nature of a resistance to insight.

It behooves us all to come to know ourselves, but it particularly behooves one whose style of defense is a distraction of attention from the center to the periphery. To engage in the pursuit of insight for EIX is to work against disconnection, robotization and self-ignorance.

I think I can make my point clear if I explain the difficulty that I had for a long time in finding jokes illustrative of the psychologically lazy character. While jokes about astute people, complainers, cowards, self-righteous people, etc., abounded, it seemed that abnegation and good adjustment had not inspired many a joke. At last, however, I realized that there is a particular type of joke that we all know which has EIX as it referent: those about idiots.

Of course, personality style is something other than intelligence, but a lack of subtlety that misses the obvious is something for which the situation of a moron is a good metaphor. Consider, for instance, the story of a man who falls from a second story with a great thump. Somebody runs toward him and, discovering that he is conscious, anxiously inquires: "Are you OK?" The answer he gets is, "I don't know, I just got here."

It is a joke about disconnection from one's experience, being "out of touch," but is this not our common predicament?

We are all relatively unconscious: imperfectly knowing what is happening in us, out of touch with our feelings, not aware of our thoughts, not even very aware of our bodies; and we can use more attention toward what we experience. To the extent that we all have a wish to not know (i.e. resistances), we can all benefit through looking inwardly. Early in our life we sensed that our experiential world was incompatible with the wishes of others and we learned to disown it. From an important point of view, psychotherapy offers us a mirror to help us see what is going on—what we feel, what we wish—and thus bring us out of confusion. To the extent that an EIX person is a specialist in playing dead, the insight medicine is particularly appropriate to him or her.

For an EVI, on the other hand, striving for self-understanding may easily become a vice. Certainly the fearful person needs insight too, and we all need to recover our natural capacity to experience, but the attainment of insight is not such a clear sign of improvement for an EVI as for an EIX. Don't we all know people who feel that they know themselves quite well, but there is nothing they can do about it? Their problem is with *doing*, not with *knowing*. And, for one who knows what to do but doesn't dare, there is the trap of wanting to make sure that there is no other way, to seek further support in the intellect when the lack is in distrusting their spontaneous promptings.

The problem of EVI is an over-inhibition of impulses. Freud's view of psychopathology as blockage of instinct surely was inspired by the EVI phenomenon, which he knew well in himself.

Suspicious-authoritarian character is over-controlled, and acts not out of organismic-intuitive promptings but in terms of reason, rules, duties, and ideals. It needs to know whether to do things this or that way, needs to know what to believe, and is excessively dependent on reference points and coordinates.

I suspect that the cultivation of spontaneity is a vehicle of no lesser importance than that of insight, and much of psychotherapy is an education in self-liberation: a learning to let go and to trust one's organism and mind—if not the world process itself.

And much of what goes on in psychotherapy is this invitation to greater freedom, beginning with Freud's free-association. It is a technique that, at the same time, removes the usual reference framework of social games and invites attention to spontaneous preferences in an attitude of non-interference. Decades later, Moreno was quite explicit in presenting psychodrama as a cultivation of spontaneity. Later yet, gestalt therapy, particularly in its group form, encouraged self-expression to a more daring degree— in a context of an organismic-taoist faith.

Anyone can be benefitted by all this, but who needs it most is the one who lives "in the head" rather than "with guts": an EVI.

Something similar may be said in regard to vain or hysterical character. Inasmuch as the EIII aspect of the universal neurosis is in each one of us—i.e., we all engage in self-falsification, deception as to who we are, confusion of our reality with our appearance—we all need authenticity. Correspondingly, much of psychotherapy, from psychoanalysis to sensitivity training and MDMA therapy,[1] is an education in authenticity. The vehicle of psychotherapy is, of course, communication—but there are degrees of communication. True communication not only leads to increasing insight, but entails an education of authenticity remedial by itself.

As with the other characters, however, what is universal is also most fitting to those in whom all psychopathology revolves around the issue of pretending or image-making. For them, it is particularly remedial to educate themselves in discriminating between what they *truly* feel, and the feelings that they *automatically* produce as part of a role. The sacrifice of the idealized self-image is likely to lead to the best results.

Let us now consider the deficiency of the perfectionistic or obsessive kind of person, and what its remedy may contribute to the psychotherapeutic need of all.

Apparently, the situation of EI is very much like that of EVI in that, in both cases, there is a lack of spontaneity—a rigidity that is the result of being too much driven by rational control and fixed schemes. The problem of EI is not a generalized inhibition or timidity, however, and its rigidity is more behavioral than intellectual. While EVI lacks that spontaneity of the mind that we may call intuition, a "feeling" for what to do for which an appropriate prescription is a "way of the heart," an EI needs to let go of an excessive control over action—putting aside the compulsion to do everything in a premeditated way and developing permissiveness in regard to impulse itself. While EVI's are so afraid of thinking certain things that would make them guilty that they may develop dis-

---

[1]MDMA is an amphetamine-related substance with effects comparable to those of MSA (which, in *The Healing Journey*, I called the "drug of analysis"), and which has particular value in removing obstacles to communication.

turbances in thinking to eschew that danger, EI is implicitly intent on avoiding behavior that has not been previously intended and passed censorship in view of a code of goodness. The most avoided behavior is, of course, the expression of anger, and correspondingly, EI people particularly benefit from re-owing this freedom through techniques as diverse as those of bioenergetics, or those developed in the 1960s by Bach in his approach to encounter groups.

That, in addition to being appropriate to the perfectionistic, the liberation of anger meets a near universal need, is echoed in the fact that it is an ubiquitous resource of eclectic (or "multi-modal") psychotherapists today; and also, in the striking benefit that people with different personality styles derive from the Hoffman Quadrinity Process, in which the catharsis of infantile rage is a major ingredient.

Let us now consider the therapeutic need of EVIII.

EVIII people harden themselves too much. It would seem that they are more animalistic than the others, but they are not; it is, rather, as if they were partisans or allies of their internal animal. They go about this in a stereotyped way, however, and this is something quite different from organismic self-regulation. The situation is that of one whose main focus has become fighting oppression; yet an anti-topdog is not an id. His "for" and "against" positions are still too much tied to childhood, being the outcome of an early adoption of intimidation as a way to overcoming obstacles. The EVIII person becomes so occupied with the war against whatever might castrate him, that he must strive for invulnerability, repressing or suppressing all weakness. Correspondingly, the therapeutic process will be one of re-sensitization, and will involve the development of tenderness.

Yet, practically, all psychotherapy entails a cultivation of love. In the case of EVIII, insensitivity is most manifest (and we may call it sadism), but in any form of neurosis there is a loss of loveability, and a hidden insensitivity. Even people who seem strikingly sensitive harbor an underlying insensitivity beneath a layer of histrionic empathy. In view of this it can be said that a universal aspect of a healing, and the return to wholeness, is the recovery of the capacity of true empathy, i.e., the development of compassion. There is a giant in the story of Pinocchio who puts Pinocchio into a cage and exploits him, and in this giant it is easy to recognize an EVIII caricature. We are told that when the giant feels compassion, he sneezes. While I don't know this form of defense to be shared by other phallic-narcissistic, the observation that compassion may be inhibited is certainly valid, and that such inhibition may support a symptom, also possible.

After having discussed the personality types mapped in the vicinity of EIX: the "benevolently" super-ego driven rigid EI, and the anti-super-ego oriented anti-social EVIII, let us move on now to ones mapped at the bottom of the Enneagram: EV and EIV. These are the neurotic styles which in the more pathological forms of expression are receiving preferential attention from psycho-analysis: the schizoid and the borderline.

Let us consider the schizoid EV first. It has been proposed that the "schizoid phenomenon" is the underlying ground of all pathologies. Guntrip, who was a disciple of Fairbairn, has elaborated on that idea, and I think that he voices a truth—but only one among several truths! For is not the ground of neurosis also the loss of the capacity to experience, the loss of authenticity, etc.? From one point of view, however, it is the "schizoid phenomenon"—i.e., a self-absorption involving the loss of relationship.

Even in the highly contactful personality of EII it is possible to find, when sincerity and self-awareness are sufficient, a schizoid layer—an incapacity to feel behind the histrionic apparatus. But the loss of relatedness is the foreground in the EV, who is an autistic person in the broad sense of the word: one isolated, relatively forgetful of the existence of the other; EV lives with a minimal capacity to know what goes on with the other. So, psychotherapy in EV will be successful when it leads to the recovery of relatedness, and this it will probably do through the unfolding of the therapeutic relationship itself. But, cannot we also address the essence of psychotherapy as a healing of contact, as gestalt therapy has?

Also in EIV, the person takes a subordinate, inferior position that involves self-frustration; but there is here a paradoxical phenomenon in that desire is not only blocked, but vehemently intensified, as if to compensate for its prohibition. One's wishes are not fulfilled, yet envy arises as a super-wish into which all the unmet wishes are transformed. As EIV heals, the person begins to do what she likes, and experiences less envy as a result of her satisfaction. The position of envy, then, is one of self-oppression and, at the same time, painful yearning. And, it is a dependent position: another must give her what she cannot give herself; the other must give her permission, appreciation, and satisfaction. It is in regard to this kind of person that Fritz Perls' statement on human growth is truest. He saw human development as a shift from dependency to autonomy. Yet, practically all of us are more or less dependent, and we need to become autonomous. From one point of view, then, psychotherapy is an overcoming of excessive dependence and the achievement of an increased self-sufficiency—and we know that this involves a shift from self-hate to self-love.

Let us now consider the personalities that we may call pseudo-social rather than anti-social, over-social or asocial: the seductive ones.

EVII, we know, is one who is excessively inclined to pleasure, but I believe that more important than the appetite for pleasure is the avoidance of pain. Much of the life of an EVII person is better described as comfortable than pleasurable: there is a reluctance to take trouble, and an avoidance of ordinary life with its difficulties. There is too much of an attitude of wanting things to come—as we say in Chile, "Like a peeled pear in the mouth." And only fantasy can give that immediate gratification; it's only a shame that it's pure fantasy.

Can it not be said that psychotherapy in general entails a reconnection with repressed or avoided pain? Psychotherapy is helping people to make contact with the pain of their past, and the pain of looking at things squarely. Acceptance of pain, we know, leads to a more satisfactory situation, for pain avoidance brings about a narrowing of consciousness and this leads to an impoverishment that, in turn, makes pain less easy to bear.

That we can all benefit from a willingness to plunge into the suffering that pervades our life experience is made evident through the success of therapies that emphasize abreaction—from primal scream to gestalt—and is deeply known to those schooled in the Gurdjieff heritage, with its emphasis in conscious suffering. The willingness to embrace the discomfort of purgatory, however, is most remedial for EVII persons, who might otherwise waste their life in the enjoyment of their talents, or the impression caused by their charm—only to end up feeling insubstantial.

The EII person, we know, is affectionate, thirsts for the love of others, and harbors a passion for being treated nicely. What is it that is missing here? While EVII disconnects from pain, EII represses the sense of lack. EII goes through life as if she or he had a surplus, in a position of false abundance sustained by a denial of frustration. Since she has to live a lie (a sort of movie), life cannot be satisfactory any more than fantasy life can, and the histrionic domain is similar to fantasy, except that it is not constituted of imaginative representations. It is, rather, an acted-out fantasy, a dramatization in the nature of a motor equivalent of fantasy (inasmuch as it replaces reality).

Supplying what is missing, then, involves reconnecting with the early sense of lack at the heart of the character. It is much easier to demand than to ask, easier to push or seduce than to feel in need. All of us have been more or less traumatized in early life; the original wound for us all has been the painful frustration of our need for love. It sometimes seems as if the EII person didn't experience such trauma, because she has always felt so lovable. What is missing for EII people, then, is to connect with their sense of insufficiency or inner poverty.

Yet, is this not part of everybody's therapeutic purgatory? Not only in the field of therapy is concentration upon the pain of separation known to be a vehicle of growth. It is a substantial part of prayer, and those willing to burn in the torment of yearning know how, paradoxically, the intensification of separation leads to unity, and concentration on frustration is known to lead to a paradoxical gratification. This is vividly apparent in the exhilaration with which an EII patient once repeated, at the end of a gestalt session: "My emptiness is my treasure!"